THE PURSUED
GENERATION

THE PURSUED GENERATION

THE GENERATION THAT WILL GIVE BIRTH TO THE RETURN OF CHRIST

DR. PAUL G. TRULIN

MORIAH PUBLICATIONS INC.®
Champlain, New York | Montréal, Canada

ISBN-13: 978-2-922189-10-0
ISBN-10: 2-922189-10-4
Publisher's Product ID: MPBKE-80005

Unless otherwise indicated, all Scripture quotations are taken from the Authorized King James Version (KJV).

Cover design by Stéphane Chauvette, Communivers / www.communivers.com

For further information, or to obtain additional copies of this publication, please contact:
Web: WWW.MORIAHPUBLICATIONS.COM   E-mail: Books@MoriahPublications.com

IN CANADA:

Legal Deposit - National Library and Archives of Canada, 2007
Legal Deposit - Bibliothèque et Archives Nationales du Québec, 2007
Canadian Copyright Registration Number: 1049522

Library and Archives Canada Cataloguing in Publication

Trulin, Paul G.
        The pursued generation : the generation that will give birth to the return of Christ! / Paul G. Trulin.

ISBN 978-2-922189-10-0

        1. Bible--Prophecies--End of the world. 2. Second Advent. 3. End of the world--Biblical teaching.
I. Title.
BT886.3.T78 2007   236'.9   C2007-904083-7

IN THE UNITED STATES OF AMERICA:

Library of Congress Cataloging-in-Publication Data

Trulin, Paul G., 1917-
        The pursued generation : the generation that will give birth to the return of Christ / Paul G. Trulin.
              p. cm.
        Summary: "A biblical study on eschatology and the last remaining generation before the coming of Christ"
--Provided by publisher.
        ISBN-13: 978-2-922189-10-0 (pbk. : alk. paper)
        ISBN-10: 2-922189-10-4 (pbk. : alk. paper)
        1. Eschatology--Biblical teaching. I. Title.

BS680.E8T78 2007
236'.9--dc22
                                    2007027187

THE PURSUED GENERATION

THE GENERATION THAT WILL GIVE BIRTH TO THE RETURN OF CHRIST

DR. PAUL G. TRULIN

TABLE OF CONTENTS

FOREWORD

This is a rich, sound and valuable study in length by a talented pastor and close friend of mine. It is a refreshing new focus on the end times. The writer is convinced, by Biblical research and penetrating observation, that there is a marked generation. He presents convincing data that "the ends of the age" must gather upon a particular and peculiar generation.

The author pursues this in both the wayward and the upward. We truly live in a whirlwind of "hastening" unequalled in history where pursuit has reached a dizzying momentum. The author sees both kingdoms, dark and light, unloosing all deterrents and heading toward the inevitable clash. Whose kingdom shall it be?

Dr. Trulin is a man of the Word. It has always been his meat. I have known him from his earliest pastoral experiences. He is a gifted teacher who has honed his extraordinary insight into the Word by teaching sundry cultures worldwide. The results will be eternal.

This volume, carefully and studiously Bible indexed, will more than replace a shelf filled with lesser works. It is prominent in my study.

The drama and romance, reduced to the bottom line, is that as God gave Eve to Adam as a <u>helper</u>, so God gave the believer to Christ. The seduction, the travesty and the warfare initiated by the adversary in both cases are Bible and history.

The author brings the reader up to date in Biblical fulfillment. Best of all... this manuscript is not a rehash of limited evangelism. Dr. Trulin, in a way I appreciate, presents the Word of God in a thud of simplicity. One does not need to be a theologian to read his message.

THE PURSUED GENERATION is <u>convincing</u>. The book is also a teachable text for any study group of any size. It avoids the speculative and deals strictly with facts. Dr. Trulin is a Bible teacher above the ordinary who never wavers, yet retains the ability to see and interpret the present.

Fortunately all the Scriptures are included with the copy. Thus one can read and study without the need of accommodating extra volumes. This book is a splendid addition to understanding "the more sure word of prophecy."

Dr. C. M. Ward

ACKNOWLEDGEMENTS

In a day when we take so many things for granted, we must always take time to remember there are many people who make things come to pass. This makes it difficult to limit our gratitude to a few. Yet, in our own lives we have all felt the warmth of gratitude towards us after we have given ourselves to help bring life and blessings to others. With this in mind, I feel deeply the need to express my feelings to some of the many people who have worked behind the scenes of my ministry.

This expression of gratitude to the following people is for their untold efforts over a period of time to make this book become a reality out of the messages I have ministered at conferences, schools of ministry, seminars and as a pastor of many years. There has been a willingness to go beyond what was asked of them to be a part of the endtime message.

In gratitude, I acknowledge the service and sacrifice of my secretary of many years, *Helen Freeman*.

In gratitude, I acknowledge the service of my former secretary, also of many years, *Bernadine Larson*.

I extend my gratitude and appreciation to my former executive secretary, *Liberty Savard*, who is now a professional Christian writer in her own ministry called *The Word Works*. She has edited and prepared the manuscript of this book with all of its many related details for printing.

Dr. Paul G. Trulin

INTRODUCTION

As you look into the history-making events that are taking place in the world today, it is clear that we are living on the edge of time. God, in His eternal Word, has foretold the future and there are unlimited mysteries being unravelled today making current events and the revealed Word of God become as one.

For eighteen centuries these mysteries, especially those in the book of Revelation and the book of Daniel, have remained largely unexplored. Today, however, many books and articles are being written as men and women are trying to unveil the meaning of these prophetic mysteries. The only book in the Bible to make promises of special blessings to everyone who reads and heeds it is the book of Revelation (Revelation 1:3).

This book you hold in your hand is not speculative. It has been written to show the accuracy of the stream of God's flow and direction today as He brings His final prophetic warnings to pass.

The eyes of the world have been upon the Middle East for a number of years. Today we are seeing the intensified work of terrorists who cannot seem to get what they want. We see the conflict in the coming together of the forces of the Arabs and the Jews. The prophecies of Ezekiel 37 referring to Russia and the kings of the North are moving into final alignment.

Our generation is looking for direction in a world that seems to be heading for self-destruction! The multitude of sermons and conferences on eschatology that have been conducted have created hunger, expectancy and confusion. The writings in this book, THE PURSUED GENERATION, have come from messages that have been born in prayer, the study of Scripture and a personal experience of living and teaching the knowledge of God's Word over many years. This book is not speculative, nor is it meant to be dramatic. Rather it is meant to bring assurance, understanding and a deep sense of direction and guidance in the endtime plan that God has for this closing generation.

In order for God to bring His eternal purpose to fulfillment through His Son, Jesus Christ, there must be a people in this generation who will go far enough to fulfill the prophetic utterances that have been so liberally given to us throughout His Word from Genesis to Revelation. John, the beloved, was exiled on the Isle of Patmos and separated from everyone but Christ. It was there that the Holy Spirit pulled the veil back and let John write the words that were revealed to him as he was caught up into the heavens. These words have been recorded for us in the Holy Bible.

The prophecies recorded in Scriptures can only be made real to you when you study the Word of God with an open heart and an open mind. In presenting the truths of the return of Christ, facts alone will not accomplish what God wants fulfilled in the lives of individuals. There must be a real anointing of the Holy Spirit upon the ministry of the Word. This quickening, the anointing of God's Spirit, is absolutely necessary for prophecy to affect the destiny and lives of men and women. This is why I have written two chapters on the unction and the anointing which breaks the yoke.

I wish to convey related truth in this book that you must lay hold of spiritually. You can read this book from two different points of understanding— spiritual or natural. You can read it as a Christian who knows what it is to be born again and who has received the incorruptible seed in your spirit which helps you to understand the direction of God's purpose for mankind.

All Christians must understand that they are not Christians because of their doctrine or what they believe; they are Christians because of what they have received... the incorruptible seed of the Spirit of Christ!

You can also read this book as one who has never experienced that relationship. The Bible's truths of Christ's second coming, its many prophecies and mysteries indiscernible to the natural mind may seem unreal to you... particularly if you do not understand that what is happening around us today has all been foretold for hundreds of years in the Word of God.

There are several patterns of understanding regarding the coming of Christ and the mysteries of the prophecies of His return, especially in the New Testament. There are many divisions among Christians as to whether Christ is coming back before, during the middle or at the end of the seven years of God's dealing with Israel. It is not the purpose of this book to enter into these different areas of understanding. Rather it is my purpose to show that when a person becomes a Christian, Christ not only cleanses him or her, but He plants the incorruptible seed of an entire new nature inside the Christian. The Bible clearly states that Christ in you is the hope of glory.

Colossians 1:13: "Who hath delivered us (YOU) from the power of darkness, and hath translated us (YOU) into the kingdom of his dear Son." Ephesians 2:1 "And YOU hath he quickened, who were dead in trespasses and sins." Colossians 1:27: "To whom God would make known what is the riches of the glory of this mystery among the Gentiles; which is Christ in YOU, the hope of glory." The purpose of Biblical prophecy is to help you to understand God's plan and purposes and to herald the soon-coming return of Christ for the people who are looking for His coming as spoken of in John 3:1-3. As you study God's Word, you can see that there are three comings of Christ. One, Jesus came into this world as a babe, the incarnation. Two, Scriptures clearly state that He is coming again for His redeemed and His holy nation, the Church. Three, the book of Revelation reveals the understanding that He is going to come back again with His redeemed saints.

From these passages, we draw a very firm conclusion that the second coming of Jesus will be in two separate events. The wrath of God, which is to be poured out upon this earth, cannot be poured out upon His Son, and from the above Scriptures we can definitely conclude that as Christians, we have the resurrected, living Christ within us. His kingdom is within our own spirit. He is alive and living within us. Before the judgments can be poured out of the wrath of God upon the endtime generation, the redeemed (not those who have just gone to church and believe in the Bible, but those who have experienced the indwelling Christ) must be taken out of this world. This "taking out" is the first event which is known and called by many as the rapture of the Church. God will not pour out His wrath upon His Son. The next dramatic event is that He will return with His saints to take over the kingdoms of this world.

There must be a people in this endtime generation who will move with God in such a way that the world will see the realities of the indwelling Christ. The world must be able to see that the power of His kingdom has taken root and is growing and spreading around the earth.

We can definitely see the two divisions of the last generation of today, just like the two crowds in Jerusalem—one followed Christ and one didn't. You can read of these two crowds in Mark 11 and Luke 23. Jesus entered Jerusalem with a fanfare of cheering and shouting; with the spreading of garments and branches of trees thrown in His path; with the people crying, "Hosannah, blessed is he that cometh in the name of the Lord." Later when Pilate wanted to set Jesus free from His accusers, the crowd screamed, "Crucify him, crucify him!" There was a division—those who were for Him and those who were against Him. In these final days, we can see the dividing of the people in this last generation—those who are marked for "rapture" and those who are marked for "judgment." Each division is marching to the beat of a different drummer and every person is either moving with Him towards the rapture or without Him towards judgment.

Now is the time to be a part of those in this endtime generation who are marked for "rapture," those who are being prepared by the Holy Spirit to enter into the fullness of what Christ has prepared for us. Remember, Jesus is coming again and the last chapter of the Bible records; "And the Spirit and the bride say, come…" When these two both speak the same language, the Shepherd is going to come! As the lambs begin to bleat, you can be sure the days of our sojourn shall be brought to the final great drama in the endtime period—the return of Christ for the "X" generation which has been marked from the beginning of time. That generation is now upon us.

Paul G. Trulin
Pastor

CHAPTER 1

WE ARE THE MARKED GENERATION

The preaching of the Gospel is the invasion of God into a hostile world—a world filled with negative forces, a world engulfed in the darkness of every act of the fallen nature of man. It is a world filled with rejection of Christ and strong resistance to the penetration of His life into the closed spirits of mankind that would create new life, purpose and peace within them.

In the history of mankind, this present generation has emerged as the most privileged and honoured of all generations since the beginning of time. This is the generation that God has marked as the "pursued generation," the generation that will give birth to the return of Christ according to the Biblical prophecies.

The length of time of a generation is speculative (from twenty to forty years or even longer), but this generation that has witnessed Israel becoming a nation again with the return of millions of Jews to their homeland is the generation referred to in God's Word. "Behold, the days come, saith the Lord, that the plowman shall overtake the reaper, and the treader of grapes him that soweth seed; and the mountains shall drop sweet wine, and all the hills shall melt. And I will bring again the captivity of my people Israel, and they shall build the waste cities, and inhabit them; and they shall plant vineyards, and drink the wine thereof; they shall also make gardens, and eat the fruit of them. And I will plant them upon their land, and they shall no more be pulled up out of their land which I have given them, saith the Lord thy God" (Amos 9:13-15).

During the last forty years our generation has also witnessed the greatest breakthroughs of human knowledge ever seen in nearly every area known to the natural man, particularly in the unfolding of the mysteries and secrets of the electronic age and space travel.

This unbelievable unveiling of scientific knowledge that has radically changed the lifestyle of every nation around the world in only a few decades staggers the imagination of even the most knowledgeable of our generation. Tremendous breakthroughs and discoveries have come in every area affecting the natural life of man such as medicine, space, communications and travel just to mention a few. In my life span, I have watched mankind move from the horse and buggy days to a generation that can travel halfway around the world in two hours. Every year has moved us forward at a rapidly increasing pace that brings the clear proof that this generation is the one spoken of in the prophetic Word as the pursued generation marked for the return of Christ.

When God wanted to reveal the future, He chose Daniel as His instrument. Daniel was a prophet with more understanding and illumination from the Spirit of God with regard to the end times than any other Old Testament writer. After all the recorded prophetic utterances in the book of Daniel, which has been the guideline for prophecy through the years, God said, "But thou, O Daniel, shut up the words, and seal the book, even to the time of the end; many shall run to and fro, and knowledge shall be increased" (Daniel 12:4). The Spirit of God opened the understanding of Daniel to look down through the telescope of time into the very day in which you and I live. We are now seeing this truth: "...many shall run to and fro, and knowledge shall be increased..." literally being fulfilled before our very eyes.

As you read the pages of this book, THE PURSUED GENERATION, it is my prayer that you will understand these endtime truths that are affecting our families, our jobs, our homes and everything else that pertains to our lives.

Each one of our lifestyles is being pressured by the realities of these last days, yet so many do not understand. Those of you who want to be on schedule with God must understand that this is the hour of harvest and ingathering, the time when the Spirit of God is moving upon all people to draw others in. This is the hour when He will prepare them not only for the return of Christ, but also to be used of Him in these final days.

Those who have studied God's Word carefully and have moved into a close relationship with Christ comprehend in their spirits that we are on the cliff's edge of spiritual breakthroughs and events that have been prophesied for hundreds of years. I am not speaking here of the many incredible events in the natural, physical world that are breaking all around us; rather I am speaking of spiritual things that are about to occur in an unprecedented pattern with astonishing spiritual results that will bring about the final harvest.

This final generation that is spoken of in the Scriptures shall see and be a part of this endtime drama. Yet, even as we live so close to this reality all around us, seeing it with our eyes, feeling it in our hearts—we can still be blind to the depths of its significance and to what the Holy Spirit is trying to tell us by the events that are taking place.

This generation, whose existence was foretold by the prophets of the Old Testament and the apostles of the New Testament as well as our spiritual forefathers, has been referred to as the "X" generation—the specific generation that will be a part of these amazing breakthroughs. Jesus, in Matthew 24 and Luke 21, defines this generation as the one that will give birth to His return. He states the different events and developments that will happen during this time.

1 Thessalonians 5 deals with the believers not being of the night and darkness and that the coming of the Lord will not overtake them like a thief in the night. Those who are believers are not "asleep" as others, but are watching and waiting. Although they do not know the exact day and the hour, believers are able to recognize the times and the seasons as referred to in the Bible.

Thus Scripture clearly defines that there is a generation that is "marked." It is the generation that will be present when the signs spoken of by Jesus in Matthew 24 and Luke 21 are finally fulfilled. Jesus clearly states that this generation shall not pass away until all these things are fulfilled. When we read of these signs in the heavens, the spiritual world and the natural world and then correlate them to present day events, it is impossible not to realize that we are on the threshold of the prophetic end of an era.

God has placed a seed of discontent into the womb of our generation that has brought many believers into the realization that there is another dimension to this life that is within us. The Holy Spirit is bringing this dimension into full development through that seed of discontent. However, far too few are actually aware of what He is doing in the hearts of those who really know Him.

This spiritual awakening of our century is the latter rain spoken of in Joel 2:23: "...for he hath given you the former rain moderately, and he will cause to come down for you the rain, the former rain, and the latter rain in the first month." There is to be a quickening, a hastening between the time of the sowing and the time of reaping the harvest. The early rain was for the preparation of the ground and the planting of the seed. The latter rain was for the finishing of the harvest that the seed would be fully developed and the heads of grain would be full and ready for use as food. We see that what is planted in one season and then harvested in another is now going to occur all at one time. Instead of the rain at the time of planting in one season and then the corresponding harvest in another season, it is now happening all in the same month.

Amos 9:13 says that the plowman will overtake the reaper and the treader of grapes will overtake him who sows the seed. This means there is going to be a coming together as one in both the sowing of the incorruptible seed of life and its development within the hearts of men and women unto its harvest. We are going to see a quickening pace in every facet of the Gospel.

Peter's prophetic utterance of the promised restoration of all things in Acts 3:19, "Repent ye therefore, and be converted, that your sins may be blotted out, when the times of refreshing shall come from the presence of the Lord," speaks of spiritual blessings. It speaks of a new move of God and His sending of Jesus Christ.

Peter was saying that before the Lord's second coming, the times of refreshing and the restoration of the power and authority and character of Christ would be manifested on earth. God's endtime plan must include a restoration of His glory, an unusual manifestation of His presence and a mighty display of His power and the gifts and fruit of the Holy Spirit. These manifestations will not only be to the Church, but through the Church to all of this generation as well.

There are some things we will see in this restorative period that can clearly be defined as already happening, such as the restoration of the nation of Israel. We can see God's dealings in the permissive patterns that the world has come to accept so casually with the rampant venereal diseases and many other deadly viruses now inflicting humanity. We will also begin to see unusual healings of afflictions in manners that we have never seen take place before.

We will find greater ministry to bring forth the understanding of the trichotomy of man as being made up of a spirit, a soul and a body. Through this understanding of these three parts of man, we will discern how God is dealing with mankind to remove the permissiveness of the world.

We will also see true spiritual leadership beginning to rise to break the yoke of the human "kingdom building" principles and patterns of carnal spiritual leaders who have dominated their churches and organizations. There is also a new kind of spiritual authority coming as we increasingly take dominion over the works of the devil and begin to bind the spirits that hold men and women in the prison cells of their own carnal natures.

The Bible says that Jesus must be retained in heaven until the time of restoration of all things which God has spoken by the mouth of His holy prophets since the world began. Peter speaks of this in his second sermon in the third chapter of Acts. His first sermon in Acts 2 was for the beginning of the Church age, while his second message in Acts 3 was for the end of the Church age. Peter says in Acts 3:21, "He (Jesus) must remain in heaven until the time comes for God to restore everything, as he promised long ago through his holy prophets."

In other words, Jesus cannot return until certain things have happened and these very things are now taking place all over the world. All around us, not only in America, but in all the nations of the world, there are events happening and things unfolding that the Bible has been foretelling for centuries. These Bible prophecies have now become the central focus of this endtime drama.

WINESKINS AND YOU

In Matthew 9:17, Jesus speaks of the wineskins which are empty, brittle and unyielding after they have been used. They once held the fruit of the wine harvest, but now they appear to be ready to be thrown out. It would seem in this illustration that the skins would be discarded, but instead of throwing the old skins away, they were recycled. The skins were submerged in water until they were soft and pliable and ready for use again. This is exactly what has been happening during this Charismatic age or period we are now in. It has been a time of teaching, worship and praise that has been received by the people of many churches with great fervour as they become soft and pliable and ready for the Master's use again.

We have been experiencing a period where the Word has been water softening the "wine skins," the individuals in the body of Christ who once held the harvest of past revivals. These skins have been and still are being prepared now to hold the fruit of the final harvest that we are about to see. This is what is happening in the world today. Every denomination is under pressure and change, under new moves of God, to remove their brittleness and soften them that they may be wineskins to hold the new wine of this last harvest, which is quickly maturing around the world.

THE TWO WORLDS

In order to understand the flow and purpose of this book, there must be a clear understanding of the two worlds we live in—the natural world and the spiritual world. We who have heard the Gospel are more acquainted with this than those who have just been newly born into the family of God or who have never known salvation. We must be the leaders, the teachers and the examples to bring reality to our generation of the things which are now taking place. It is our responsibility to acquaint them with the truth that we are all involved with these two worlds, the spiritual and the natural. We must show them how God's people are moving farther and farther away from the natural world and into a new dimension of life, authority and dominion through the spiritual world.

The natural world has produced a way of life that has been removing all of the "ancient landmarks." The Old Testament is very clear regarding the importance of the ancient landmarks and how God expected people to respect them. "Cursed be he that moveth his neighbour's landmark" (Deuteronomy 27:17). "Remove not the ancient landmarks, which thy fathers have set" (Proverbs 22:28). These landmarks were to be established and then left untouched. We are living in dangerous times when we need to "know that we know" that God's Word is the cornerstone of all truth... the ancient landmark that can be trusted implicitly.

In our society, the "ancient landmarks" of the Word have been widely disregarded for some time. The Word has established the landmarks which set the boundary lines of honesty, decency, family standards, the sanctity of marriage vows and spiritual lifestyles. These landmarks have all been moved about in permissiveness by man until the world of today has no idea where the limits are. It is only within the guidelines and the "landmarks" of the Word that God can bless... when we move outside of these guidelines, we move out of God's divine boundaries into the enemy's territory. It is within the enemy's land that disobedience, sin, regressions in morality, and the destructive lifestyles of so much of the world's society is being produced today.

It is very easy to feel like a ship without a compass, driven by the winds of change, as the principles and standards that have made our natural life seem secure are dissolving all around us and other arenas of control are emerging. The standards of marriage, home and family as well as the characteristics of loyalty, honesty, morality and integrity are all increasingly giving way to the lower level of human nature in the world. Many Christians are accepting the flood tide of the carnal patterns of religion today—settling for a spiritually weakened, humanistic quality of life instead of the submitted, obedient, spiritual life of higher quality and power.

The church world has also had an overemphasis on spiritual and Scriptural "knowledge" as being all that is needed without the knowledge ever being turned into actual spiritual experience and reality. This has produced multitudes of "Bible experts" who have never entered into the real life stream and flow of God which is "Christ in you—the hope of glory."

The motivational level of mankind in general has sharply departed from its former sense of honour in providing for oneself and family through a teaching to be productive in this world. It has decreased to a lower level of "survival" which is costing our government and states untold billions of dollars in financial and material aid. Why? Spiritual motivation has diminished until the motivation of human survival has come down to the level where millions do not care beyond the point of a roof above their heads, food on the table and a television set. All of this speaks of the ways of the natural man. When natural man loses the motivational quality in his life, he succumbs to a spirit of discouragement, despondency, and helplessness—bowing to his circumstances, seeking the easiest and often lowest way out.

The world we live in is governed and pressured by the endtime happenings as prophesied in 2 Timothy 3:1-4, "This know also, that in the last days perilous times shall come. For men shall be lovers of their own selves, covetous, boasters, proud, blasphemers, disobedient to parents, unthankful, unholy, without natural affection, trucebreakers, false accusers, incontinent, fierce, despisers of those that are good, traitors, heady, high-minded, lovers of pleasures more than lovers of God." This refers to the lifestyle of men and women in the latter days. The condition of their "inner man" is reflected in their outward actions. We see these four Scriptures written to Timothy by the Apostle Paul as if they were being read on the front pages of today's newspapers.

The level of one's natural life is based upon his or her relationship with Christ. It is this relationship alone that will enable each one of us to rise above the pressures all around us that are trying to alienate us from the real quality of life that makes Christianity attractive to the world. It is this relationship that will bring God's restoration principles fully into action in these last days.

The church world that has its beginnings in great spiritual awakening has been in a regressive pattern almost since its inception until it has become more like the natural world than the spiritual world. The purpose of the enemy's pressures today is that the Gospel, which has brought forth powerful results and established great things for the kingdom of God through spiritual principles, should move into the patterns of the world. The regressive patterns that have moved upon the Church have become reflected in every aspect of our lives, our homes, our families, our marriages, our jobs and our spiritual lives.

Many speak freely of God, the death and resurrection of Jesus and the coming of the Holy Spirit; but the truths provided by this divine Trinity are not always a living reality in the religious systems of our day. What once was clear-cut, pure Christianity is today becoming closer to man-made religious trends which are not of God. Rather they can be classified as "another gospel" as stated in the first chapter of Galatians. The world's patterns have established a church system that operates and promotes itself by the same means as the world system promotes and develops itself. Gradually there has been a turning away from the secrets of Gospel preaching, Gospel ministry and Gospel service until "spirituality" is more sense knowledge than the revelation knowledge that comes only from the work of the Spirit of God. Often there is no emphasis at all on the anointing or unction of the Spirit of God in the Gospel.

THE SPIRITUAL WORLD

In our understanding we must come to the realization that the spiritual world is as real as the natural world. We have lived so much in the natural world that our lifestyle may become governed more by natural laws than spiritual laws from God's Word if we do not have a clear awareness of the difference between the two. This is why it is important to be in the Word and in prayer and in fellowship of the body of Christ, to keep our spiritual sensitivity and balance. It is very easy to develop attitudes and ideas that are contrary to God's Word because of the inclinations of our own thinking and the ever present, pervasive influence of the world around us. We must constantly be feeding our spiritual man with the things of God while, at the same time, we are starving or crucifying our old carnal nature. We must deny our carnal nature the things of the world that would strengthen its power to entice us with the lusts of the flesh.

Some of the root causes of the tragedy of the drug and the dope epidemic of our times have come out of the deep cry of this generation that knows there is something more in the spiritual world than they have in the natural world. Many have tried to get a spiritual experience by entering through false doors. In their spirits they are reaching for God, but He cannot be reached through man's own efforts or through mind altering chemical substances. Those who would enter into a true, life changing, peace giving and spiritual experience must come solely through the Spirit of God.

One will not find the answer to this deep cry and need that is being expressed in the actions of this generation in man-made, soul-oriented, religious systems. If man is to find the answer to the cry and the hunger that lies within, he will have to find it by moving beyond the soulish realm of his mind, will and emotions. He is going to have to move beyond the gratification of the dictates of his body. He is going to have to enter into the realm of understanding that he is made up of spirit, soul and body. God is a Spirit, man is a spirit and Satan is a spirit. If we are going to have life changes that are for time and eternity, we must build them within the spirit part of man. Soulish religion is a thief that has stolen the true relationship with God from millions of men and women.

Much of the church world that has come forth out of great spiritual revivals, renewals and restorations has, over a period of time, reverted back to man-made religious systems. The doctrines may be the same, the preaching may seem the same, the cry of the heart is the same… but the supernatural is missing. The supernatural factor that only God can put into the preaching of the Gospel is the unction of the Holy One which is really the anointing of the Holy Spirit. It is this unction that brings the presence and the power of God into a service and into the spirits of men and women. This divine unction is the one distinguishing feature that separates true Gospel preaching from all other methods of teaching and presenting information. The unction makes truth alive and penetrating. It illuminates the Word and quickens the intellect and empowers it to apprehend what the Word of God is saying. Without the unction, the Gospel has no more power to propagate itself than any other system of sharing information. The unction on the ministry of the Word puts God into the Gospel and without it, the Gospel is left to the carnal forces of talent, ingenuity and manipulation by men and women seeking to lay their religious concepts and doctrines upon mankind.

Because of this tendency of the natural man to inject himself into the Gospel, many great moves of God have culminated in denominations that moved for a period of time with God, but then gradually regressed to carnal motivations. The spiritual characteristics that came forth out of these mighty movements ultimately diminished as well until their means of presenting the Gospel faded into man's patterns.

The supernatural life stream of God is missing in much of the church world today and the people are dissatisfied, yet they do not know what to do about it. They remain members of their churches, but they are not involved in soul winning, in the final harvest or in the propagation of the Gospel. The death patterns have become clear and distinct within much of the religious system today.

When there have been times of refreshing with the outpouring of the Spirit of God, many of these churches were touched. But when they would not turn and move out in a new direction with God, there came a gleaning within the systems of religion to meet the cry of the seeking hearts and to establish a people that God could use. Out of that gleaning came what has become known as the Pentecostal movement.

This gathering up and gleaning that became the Pentecostal movement has splintered into several different Pentecostal church groups, as well as some other denominational churches that now emphasize the Holy Spirit. We have seen many marvellous things take place such as tremendous missionary activity, numerical growth, larger churches, miracles, television and radio ministries, a greater choice of Gospel recordings, expanded teachings,

27

videos and cassettes until the Charismatic movement (as it is also known) has circulated around the world. But the same forces of regression that caused other denominations to move out of God's divine plan and purpose are now operating within those who were originally gleaned out of the religious systems to form the Pentecostal movement.

We find the Holy Spirit is now "gleaning the gleanings" in order to bring a restoration of all things as spoken of in the third chapter of Acts in Peter's second sermon. The Holy Spirit is bringing forth a renewed realization of the power and the marvellous works of Jesus which have been neglected by a lack of moving deep enough into God. The entire body of Christ was intended to exercise the five ministry gifts that Christ gave to the Church (Ephesians 4). These gifts were given so that God might have a vehicle to carry out the purpose for which Christ died, the Holy Spirit came and the Word was written. God must have a people to bring the message of His life, healing, restoration, love and power back into the world.

GOD GAVE TWO GIFTS TO THIS WORLD

God established a divine pattern in His redemptive plan. In order to reach the dead spirits of unregenerated men and women, He had to first bring them to life. This meant that Jesus had to come into the world. The life of the Father was placed into Jesus as a babe to be humanized, and then thoroughly tested in His human body to meet all the circumstances of daily living… every situation, every temptation, every heartache and every need. This life was tried and tested in His body, soul and spirit so that not one situation or need could arise in your life and mine that it had not already overcome.

When Jesus was crucified and His body lay in the tomb, His Spirit left His body and went down into the regions of the damned, straight to the throne room of Satan. Jesus went to take back from Satan the keys of the kingdom, the very keys that Adam had given to Satan when he surrendered his authority and dominion in the Garden of Eden. Christ's victorious life, which is in the incorruptible seed that was planted in you, has every key of victory and overcoming that you will ever need in order to walk in righteousness as a Christian.

TWO GIFTS FROM GOD

God gave us the gift of life through His Son. 1 John 5:11-12 says, "And this is the record, that God hath given to us eternal life, and this life is in his Son. He that hath the Son hath life; and he that hath not the Son of God hath not life." Ephesians 2:1 says, "And you hath he quickened, who were dead in trespasses and sins." This is the gift of life that man was to experience.

The second gift was the Holy Spirit, "that ye might receive power after the Holy Spirit has come upon you." This was not only for power in our lives, but it was a gift to reveal Christ in all that He is… that the crucified and resurrected Christ with all of His attributes as spoken of in the Gospel would become a part of our lives by the work of the Holy Spirit within us.

God has given these two, inseparable gifts to us… the gift of His Son and the gift of the Holy Spirit. This is an area where the body of Christ needs clarification and understanding. Much of the weakness in many Christians today is not because of wrong doctrine, it is because of a lack of emphasis on that which produces and maintains life. We can overemphasize one important area and underemphasize another one until we create a spiritual imbalance. This imbalance produces a prime area for the enemy to introduce regressive factors that begin to take hold within individuals as well as within the corporate body of Christ. I would like to illustrate this with a personal experience that awakened me to a reality that has affected my entire life.

As a young person, I dreamed of one day becoming first an attorney and then a judge. When I completed high school, I began taking law courses and reading everything I could lay hold of to gain as much legal knowledge as possible. Almost everything I did was directed towards the ultimate purpose of going full-time to law school. This was during the depression and I moved from North Dakota to Los Angeles looking for a means to enter law school. Not finding any opportunities there, I moved to Oregon to live with my mother's uncle. This was God's way of bringing me back into the family of God that I had pulled away from.

As early as my teenage years, I knew the call of God was on me for full-time ministry. I refused to acknowledge it even under strong dealings by the Holy Spirit within my life. A deep crisis in my life and our family occurred when my mother was at death's door and the doctors said she would not live. There at her bedside, with other members of the family, I made a surrender to God that instantly brought a quickening to my mother's body and her recovery.

I was deeply aware of the commitment that I had finally made and the results it had brought, yet I was unsure how to fulfill that commitment. God still had to bring me to a place of further surrender. I worked for a printing company in Portland, Oregon, and as I began to attend church again, God moved me into an unusual experience and I was filled with the Holy Spirit. Then a door suddenly opened through a friend of the family and the tuition was paid for me to attend Northwest Bible College in Seattle under Dr. Henry H. Ness.

Upon graduation, under the call of God and with a deep sense of yearning to enter into the field of missions, I surrendered that yearning to God and became a pastor. God blessed me with growth, building programs, ministry in conferences and seminars; but twenty years later I had come to the end of myself. I did not want to pastor anymore and something had to happen in my own life.

Things were not clear, but I began to see the two lives, the natural and the spiritual life. I began to weigh one against the other. I began to realize that there were two gifts, the gift of life and the gift of the Holy Spirit, but I could not put them all together. I became painfully aware that what we as Christians were teaching and preaching was too far apart from what we were living. There were pieces missing.

Something had to happen; I had to find an answer in order to be honest with God and with His people. I had just taken a church in Sacramento, California, and had only been there a few weeks when I cried out to God, "Lord, I can't go through with this!" I had left a large, comfortable church to take this small church full of struggles, problems and heartaches and, after three weeks, I planned to resign on the fourth Sunday.

I did not tell my family of my plans, but it was on the following Wednesday night before a small handful of people that I heard God speak audibly to me for the second time in my life, as clearly as you could speak to me. It penetrated my spirit and left me without a doubt and without any questions. The words He spoke to me were, "I will build my church and the gates of hell shall not prevail against it if you will let me and if you will know me in the power of my resurrection." These were the words spoken to Peter in Matthew 16 when Christ asked Peter if he knew who He was.

I knew the Holy Spirit had awakened me to the missing link, the weakness, the underemphasis that was in my ministry and in the church world. I began to see that for years the sincere Pentecostal movements had placed their emphasis heavily upon the Holy Spirit, but had neglected another area that the Holy Spirit anoints so strongly. This is the important area of understanding and knowing the resurrection life of Jesus which brought us into spiritual life in the first place so that the Holy Spirit can indwell and anoint us.

The following Sunday I entered into a new ministry, I preached with an anointing that I had never had before, with a joy that I had never experienced before, with a peace that excelled anything I felt in the past, and with an intenseness and excitement that changed the whole pattern of my ministry. I had ministered many times on the gifts of the Spirit, but now I understood God's distinctively different, yet dependent upon each other, gifts to the world... the gift of His Son and the gift of the Holy Spirit.

THE TWO KINDS OF KNOWLEDGE

The breakthroughs that came in my own life brought understanding that also showed me the two kinds of knowledge, sense knowledge and revelation knowledge. Sense knowledge is the knowledge we receive through our five senses of seeing, hearing, tasting, feeling and smelling. These five senses are the avenues through which we receive our natural knowledge. But natural knowledge will not reveal Christ, who is a Spirit, nor will it unveil His life within us by the Holy Spirit. I began to understand that only revelation knowledge, as revealed by the Holy Spirit in the Word of God, could reveal Christ to our hearts.

God hid His life in the Word. The Holy Spirit must unveil and communicate this reality into our spirits in order for that life which is hidden in Christ to become a part of us. As I began to recognize these facts, I also understood how the Christian world can regress if it does not understand and enter into these principles. God has His own way of protecting His divine truth, and if it is followed in the pattern that He has ordained, it will give life. If it is not followed in His pattern, it will bring death, decay and alienation. We see this clearly illustrated in the fifth chapter of Hebrews.

The author of the book of Hebrews had to be a Jew who knew the law better than anyone in that day, someone who had been converted from Judaism to Christianity. He also had to have had a powerful experience with Christ that could build the bridge between the law and grace, a bridge of deep understanding between the "old" and the "new" covenants. It is without question that the Apostle Paul was that person, the one whose apostleship had been declared by Christ Himself.

The Hebrew Christians had undergone great persecution and they were beginning to forsake the assembling of themselves together which is so important for spiritual growth. Having alienated themselves from many of the comforting factors of being a part of the commonwealth of Israel with its patterns of spiritual life and strong culture, there was a regression taking place within these believers as they looked longingly back towards the "security" of their former lifestyle.

In Hebrews 5:11 Paul begins to address their situation, "Of whom (Jesus) we have many things to say, and hard to be uttered, seeing ye are dull of hearing. For when for the time ye ought to be teachers, ye have need that one teach you again which be the first principles of the oracles of God; and become such as have need of milk, and not of strong meat" (Hebrews 5:11-12). Meat speaks of maturity; milk speaks of beginners or of babes in Christ. "For every one that useth milk is unskillful in the word of righteousness; for he is a babe. But strong meat belongeth to them that are of full age, even those who by reason of use have their senses exercised to discern both good and evil" (Hebrews 5:13-14).

This is very descriptive of what is happening in the church world today because of compromises and promiscuous living. People are letting God's Word be put aside and human reasoning take its place. Christians are living in patterns that are contrary to the divine pattern of true life in God's Word. This is proof that spiritual life is not in development as many of these Christians are living under standards set up and compromised by man's thinking instead of God's Word.

As I moved into this new realm of ministry and teaching, I began to teach these truths to others through special Thursday morning "Life in the Spirit" services that I conducted weekly for the next twenty years. Multitudes of people were quickened and blessed by these truths and revelations. Out of these morning teaching sessions came three books, THE MAKING OF A CHRISTIAN, MY BODY–HIS LIFE and RESURRECTION LIFE.

These books, particularly MY BODY–HIS LIFE with hundreds of thousands of copies in print, have been translated into a number of languages. These books are now circulating in more than sixty nations of the world. It is also my privilege to teach these truths, known as the message of the Christ life, in World Evangelism's Schools of Ministry throughout the nations of the world.

As we understand the two natures, death and life, we then become aware of how we need to pray and feed the life nature by emphasizing these truths... as well as how we must avoid feeding the death nature. If we want the life nature to grow strong, we starve the death nature. When we feed the death nature, we starve the life nature.

The first work of God's redemption is cleansing, forgiveness of sins and the planting of the seed of life into our spirits. The second work of redemption is through the work of the Holy Spirit to give power for service so that supernatural acts will be manifested through God's people to a doubting world that rejects the Gospel.

As the realization of these two gifts becomes clear in our spiritual understanding, a new life will emerge within the church that will swallow up the deadness and emptiness that has developed within the religious systems of today. There will come forth the power and the force within the invincible body of Christ that is going to rule and reign with Him.

These important truths that I have shared with you can energize and revitalize your spiritual life. They have come out of years of ministry and prayer, years of seeking and reaching for breakthroughs and an understanding of the things that have been neglected and have thereby created weaknesses within the people of God. These truths have been like keys to open previously closed doors, like putting a chain together with the missing link now in place... they have tied together the truths in God's Word that do not work independently, but work powerfully together.

HOW IMPORTANT ARE THESE TRUTHS TO THIS PURSUED GENERATION?

This is the generation that is going to give birth to the return of Christ as spoken of prophetically in God's Word. For this to happen, there are certain things that must transpire spiritually in this generation for it to fulfill its destiny.

Over the past few years, an understanding of the meaning of the word "generation" has begun to come into focus. The word generation is a descriptive word that refers to a span of time. It is difficult to assign an exact number of years that a generation refers to, but we can draw some idea. In one part of the Old Testament a generation is spoken of as twenty or twenty-five years. In other parts of the Bible it can be interpreted as the lifespan of Jesus of thirty-three years. Some Bible scholars believe it means forty years and some interpret it as seventy years. The generally accepted pattern is that a generation is approximately forty years.

The Bible is clearly pointing towards a period of time in which the endtime prophecies are to be fulfilled. It states very clearly in Matthew 24, Mark 13 and Luke 21 that when this period of final prophecies begins, the generation of that time would not pass away until all is fulfilled. When this generation sees these things coming to pass, they are to know that the summer is nigh and the harvest is ready. The generation living at that time will not pass away until all is fulfilled.

We are a part of this pursued generation, the final generation of this world that is now being brought into a greater depth of the revelation of Christ. This generation is the vehicle in His hands that will reach the world by bringing awakening to churches, Christians, ministers and leaders. This awakening is not coming only by supernatural miracles and by spiritual blessings... it will not come only by greater emphasis on evangelization... it will come forth having been born within our spirits.

It is humanly impossible for a worldwide spiritual awakening to take place only through the efforts of men and women awakened by the Spirit to the realization that Jesus is coming. But if you understand the Word and the Spirit of the Word, you will clearly see that the last chapter of Revelation speaks of the spirit and the bride of Christ saying, "Come", and that only then will Jesus come. This infers that there will be such an invasion of the Spirit of God into the spirits of men and women that it will bring an illumination and awakening like the world has never seen or comprehended since the day of Pentecost in the upper room.

As you read these pages, I pray that you are becoming firmly aware of two inseparables: the resurrection life of Jesus and the work of the indwelling Holy Spirit. As this becomes clearer in our understanding, we will see how vital they both are in bringing all Christians and the Church into alignment with God's divine pattern. We must fully realize how these two inseparables work together to not only maintain our spiritual life, but to increase it.

The resurrection life of Christ and the work of the indwelling Holy Spirit operating together within believers will create such a life flow of God in us and through us that His Church will become an invincible force that nothing can deter. It will become the anointed reality that will penetrate every corner of the darkness of this age. As this generation, we are going to be the cutting edge in bringing about the breakthroughs and final events that will bring forth the return of Christ in our day.

We must be aware that there will be great changes in the world both spiritually and materially. There will be upheavals of all kinds as well as resistance like we have never seen before. By reading the Word of God it is clear that what took place before the last week of Jesus' earthly life was Satan's turning all hell loose to defeat Him and thereby block the greatest event ever to occur in mankind's history. Satan's mission was to press Christ into disobedience, that He would not fulfill the Father's plan for His life. But Jesus prevailed and brought forth what you and I have today—a new life, a new tomorrow, a new nature and eternity with God.

In these final days just prior to Christ's return, we can expect every force of the enemy both on the earth and in the heavenlies to be resistant, hostile and destructive to the cause of the Gospel. It will not only be a visible resistance, but it will be subtle and "invisible" as well; bringing alienation, deceptive appetites and strange attitudes that can only be discerned and attacked spiritually. The religious world will oppose the spiritual world. There will be churches (of many established denominations) that have diminished in their spiritual life flow until they will hinder more than help the cause of the Gospel because they have built their spirituality around themselves instead of around Jesus.

There is one thing you can rest assured of... Jesus is coming! He is going to rapture an awakened Church, a refined-by-fire Church, a strong Church—He is going to have a Church without spot or wrinkle. So, remember, you may already be facing obstacles and misunderstandings, you may have already entered into areas that you do not comprehend and you may wonder if you are standing all alone. But Jesus is going to come right on schedule and the Spirit of God is moving everyone to that precise point in time. One of these days the greatest unveiling that you have ever witnessed in your life will happen within Christianity and you will see a Church rise up like it has been born again overnight... just like you will see Israel when their blindfolds are taken off and they shall behold their Messiah.

CHAPTER 2

BIRTH OF A KINGDOM

As you begin to read this chapter, I want you to understand a dimension of truth that is clearly defined in the Scriptures, yet often neglected. Throughout the Old Testament the lineage pattern is after the natural man. Old Testament Scripture had to deal with man in his natural state because his spirit which once had communion with God (but was lost through Adam's sin) was no longer the dwelling place of God. It is as if spiritual blinds were pulled and remained as such until the birth of Christ and His resurrection which would open the spirits of men and women which had been closed to fellowship with God throughout these centuries.

As the birth of Christ is recorded in the beginning of the New Testament, we find the beginning of a new kingdom established by Jesus Christ. I hope to build a bridge for you between these two divine patterns that will help you to see God's transition from the natural to the spiritual.

From the time of Adam until the coming of Christ in human form on earth, man's spirit was alienated from God. God had to create a plan to reinhabit man. The New Testament is no longer the pattern of man being under the law as in the Old Testament, but instead it is a new and living way where man's spirit can be inhabited by God again. No longer was man to live by the outward patterns of the law, but instead by the law of the Spirit of life in Christ Jesus (Romans 8:2) dwelling within him. Men and women would not know Christ in the flesh or in the Old Testament pattern—they could now know Him as the crucified, resurrected spiritual Christ who would dwell within them.

When a person becomes a Christian, he or she is born into the kingdom of God's dear Son as clearly stated in Colossians 1:13, "Who hath delivered us from the power (or kingdom) of darkness, and hath translated us into the kingdom of his dear Son." When this takes place in the New Testament era, it definitely divides all who would live from the time of His birth until the time of His return into two kingdoms or divisions—one that is marching toward the rapture and one that is marching toward judgment. As you continue to read this chapter on "The Birth of a Kingdom," it will become very plain that one division of people known as the redeemed live by a new nature birthed by the seed of a new life planted into their spirits. The other division of this generation, from the time of Christ's resurrection until His return, live by the fallen nature of Adam.

In this book, THE PURSUED GENERATION, when reference is made to our generation which will give birth to the return of Christ, remember that there are these two different parts to this generation. One part has had the seed of a new nature planted into their spirits to become alive unto God, and one part still lives by the fallen nature of Adam. The seed of a new life, that incorruptible seed as spoken of in 1 Peter 1:23, has never entered into their spirits. They have never become a part of the chosen generation, the royal priesthood, the holy nation, the peculiar people in the prophetic words of Peter (1 Peter 2:9).

Again I entreat you to consider these tremendous transitions in understanding how the Christ without becomes the Christ within when Christians are translated out of the kingdom of darkness into the kingdom of God's dear Son (Colossians 1:13).

Jesus began to penetrate the understanding of His disciples shortly before the crucifixion with regard to this transition. In chapter sixteen of the Gospel of John, you will notice that He introduces this penetration further with the statement, "A little while, and ye shall not see me: and again, a little while, and ye shall see me, because I go to the Father" (John 16:16). They did not understand what He was talking about and began to ask questions. Jesus knowing the struggle they were in spoke to them that for a little while—not a long period of time—but for a short period of time they would not see Him. Then He explained, "Verily, verily, I say unto you, that ye shall weep and lament, but the world shall rejoice: and ye shall be sorrowful, but your sorrow shall be turned into joy. A woman when she is in travail hath sorrow, because her hour is come: but as soon as she is delivered of the child, she remembereth no more the anguish, for joy that a man is born into the world. And ye now therefore have sorrow: but I will see you again, and your heart shall rejoice, and your joy no man taketh from you" (John 16:20-22).

He is trying to tell them that they knew Him by the flesh which was being prepared to pass away... His eyes, His face, His form. But now they were going to know Him as the crucified, resurrected Christ in their spirits—the indwelling Christ. They would know Him in their spirit—a spirit that was no longer dead but now was alive unto God. Their joy would be full because no one could take it away from them. He also said, "Whatsoever you ask the Father in my name, He will give it to you." Here we find the tremendous significance of the Christ of the flesh which was formerly without now about to become the Christ within. They would no longer know Him after the flesh, but they would know Him by who He really was within their spirit.

With this revelation in the hearts of the disciples, Jesus left them and went on to Jerusalem. When He went into the temple, He found the Jews violating God's ordinances; they had lost the true meaning of what the temple was to represent. They had reverted to the natural, to man's way of doing things.

Jesus was preparing to become the Christ within, the Christ who would enter into the very spirits of men and women. He knew that He had to awaken them, to bring them to the point of even deep resentment and reaction in order to motivate those of the Sanhedrin and the religious system of the day. He literally brought on Himself the crisis situation which was to prepare the way for His crucifixion that He could finish His work on earth. He was developing the beginning of the great transition from the Christ without to the Christ within.

39

Luke recorded Jesus' words when He went into the temple in Jerusalem, "And he went into the temple, and began to cast out them that sold therein, and them that bought; saying unto them, It is written, My house is the house of prayer; but ye have made it a den of thieves. And he taught daily in the temple. But the chief priests and the scribes and the chief of the people sought to destroy him, and could not find what they might do: for all the people were very attentive to hear him" (Luke 19:45-48).

Matthew said, "And (Jesus) said unto them, It is written, My house shall be called the house of prayer: but ye have made it a den of thieves. And the blind and the lame came to him in the temple; and He healed them. And when the chief priests and scribes saw the wonderful things that He did, and the children crying in the temple, and saying, Hosanna to the son of David; they were sore displeased" (Matthew 21:13-15).

The temple that was built for God's glory had become man-centered. Jesus went into the temple and turned over the tables of the money changers, using a whip to drive them and the other merchants out of His Father's house of prayer. This greatly angered the chief priests and scribes as well as the merchants.

How does this apply today? An old pattern was being closed and an entirely different, new pattern was being formed here. There is a mystery that is referred to in Romans 11 which speaks of the old and the new. In studying this chapter, we can refresh our understanding of the birth of Christ's kingdom.

In Romans 11 God is referred to as the real olive tree, the root, the strength and the life-giving force behind both Israel and the redeemed—the body of Christ. God is the same in the Old Testament as He is in the New Testament, but His means of expressing Himself are different. In disobedience and disbelief, Israel (as the natural branches) was cut off from the olive tree. They were blinded in part from seeing the truth so that the Gentiles might be grafted in. God did not have an expression of Himself through His people during this time between the cutting off of the old branches and the grafting in of the new ones.

God has to have some expression of Himself in the world. In the Old Testament He spoke by incidences such as the crossing of the Red Sea, Daniel in the lion's den, the three Hebrew children in the furnace, Israel's protection from the plagues and their deliverance out of Egypt. God also spoke and demonstrated who He was through individuals. Israel would fear their God and serve for a time, but then in times of blessing they would become careless and indifferent again because their nature was still the old nature that Adam had brought down into death.

In the Old Testament it was by the law, by the prophets and by men and women used of God that God's message was expressed to mankind. These men and women of God were not indwelt by the Spirit of God, rather the Spirit would come upon them and they would give forth what God wanted to communicate to Israel at that time. As He began to move into a new, divine invasion of indwelling man through the planting of the incorruptible seed, God was creating a new avenue through which He would express Himself to the world—the Spirit indwelt body of Christ, the Church.

Hebrews 1:1-2 says, "God, who at sundry times and in divers manners spake in time past unto the fathers by the prophets, hath in these last days spoken unto us by his Son, whom he hath appointed heir of all things, by whom also he made the world." Here again we see the old and the new. How does God bridge the tremendous gap that lies between the law and the grace of the indwelling life of Christ?

Paul built a bridge for us as he wrote to the Romans of how the Israelites, by their unbelief, were cut off and blinded in part that the Gentiles might be grafted into the olive tree. Paul warned that they, too, could be cut off if they became careless and indifferent like Israel did. We, as Gentiles, are referred to as wild and contrary by nature, yet we are grafted into the good olive tree, which is God Himself, where the natural branches were cut off.

In the New Testament, Jesus came to bring a new life into the old, wild olive branch. This new nature was going to begin from a seed which was to be Jesus as spoken of in Genesis 3:15 and also in Galatians 3:16. God's way of rehabilitating fallen man was not only by His laws, but by the placing of a new nature inside man's spirit. This new nature would be fully formed within him according to Galatians 4:19 so that man could live by the life of another.

THE LAW COULD NOT GIVE LIFE

To further understand the patterns of truth that were introducing the change that was to come—the forming of a new kingdom—we need to review certain Scriptures. Galatians 3:13-14, "Christ hath redeemed us from the curse of the law, being made a curse for us; for it is written, Cursed is every one that hangeth on a tree; that the blessing of Abraham might come on the Gentiles through Jesus Christ; that we might receive the promise of the Spirit through faith." Jesus became the curse so that we who would accept His gift of life would no longer have to be under the curse of the law. We receive the promise of the Spirit because of faith that was imparted to us.

Galatians 3:19-21, "Wherefore then serveth the law? It was added because of transgressions, till the seed (Jesus) should come to whom the promise was made; and it was ordained by angels in the hand of a mediator... Is the law then against the promises of God? God forbid; for if there had been a law given which could have given life, verily righteousness should have been by the law." The law could not give life.

These scriptures show us the beginning of the framework of change, the building of a bridge from the old to the new... the new kingdom, an unshakable kingdom. "At that time His (God's) voice shook the earth, but now he has promised, 'Once more I will shake not only the earth but also the heavens.' The words 'once more' indicate the removing of what can be shaken—that is, created things—so that what cannot be shaken will remain. Therefore, since we are receiving a kingdom that cannot be shaken, let us be thankful, and so worship God acceptably with reverence and awe, for our God is a consuming fire" (Hebrews 12:26-29 NIV).

Jesus brought the change that was to build a new way—the new kingdom. The old was dying and the new was rising. God's plan that began before the earth was born has continued right up until now and will continue on past the end of time. We are not a drifting humanity, we are a people headed in a direction... we are part of God's plan.

THE TWO WORLDS MEET

Luke 2:25, "And, behold, there was a man in Jerusalem, whose name was Simeon; and the same man as just and devout, waiting for the consolation of Israel; and the Holy Ghost was upon him." The setting here is of an aged man who had studied the law carefully and who knew there was a Messiah to come. Simeon had prayed through the years and now he was old and his steps were feeble. He knew his days were numbered, but God had given him a promise that the Messiah would come in his lifetime. Then this aged saint was drawn by the Holy Spirit to come to the temple.

"And it was revealed unto him by the Holy Ghost, that he should not see death, before he had seen the Lord's Christ. And he came by the Spirit into the temple..." (Luke 2:26-27). No rabbi or teacher told him and the law didn't tell him, but it was the Spirit of God who told him to go to the temple. There was something about to happen that he had prayed and longed for over many years.

"...And he came by the Spirit into the temple, and when the parents brought in the child Jesus, to do for him after the custom of the law, then took he him up in his arms..." (Luke 2:27). This aged man, a prophet of the Lord, reached out and took the baby Jesus into his arms. Simeon represents the old, the law. He stood holding in his arms the beginning of the new kingdom. He blessed God and then said, "...Lord, now lettest thou thy servant depart in peace, according to thy word; for mine eyes have seen the salvation which thou hast prepared before the face of all the people, a light to lighten the Gentiles, and the glory of thy people Israel" (Luke 2:29-32).

Here Simeon bridged the gap between the old and the new, between the law and grace that would be the redemption of mankind... and also between the Gentile and the Jew. He stood with the baby Jesus in his arms and in complete fulfillment asked God to now let him die and depart in peace because he had seen the beginning of the new and he was the fading of the old.

Here is the law and here is grace for the redemption of mankind. Romans 8:2-4 says, "For the law of the Spirit of life in Christ Jesus hath made me free from the law of sin and death. For what the law could not do, in that it was weak through the flesh, God sending his own Son in the likeness of sinful flesh, and for sin, condemned sin in the flesh; that the righteousness of the law might be fulfilled in us, who walk not after the flesh, but after the Spirit." We are free.

Now notice in Colossians 1:13, "Who hath delivered us from the power of darkness, and hath translated us into the kingdom of his dear Son." God delivered us out of the power of darkness and translated us into the new kingdom which did not exist until Jesus came. Before Jesus came, there were many different kinds of life existing in the world... biological life, plant life, animal life... but there was no divine life (called "zoe" in the Greek) flowing in the world until He came. Jesus brought a new life flow with Him into this world.

This divine life flow was not experienced in the Old Testament because Adam sacrificed it by his disobedience in the Garden. Adam and Eve were given choices in the Garden of Eden. God wanted man to have the right of choice for He has never wanted robots who would serve Him mindlessly. He wants your love and your obedience because you choose to give them to Him. God told Adam he was forbidden to partake of the Tree of Knowledge of good and evil. He did not tell him that if he ate of the Tree of Life, he would live forever. However, everything in the Garden with the one exception of the Tree of Knowledge was available to them... including the Tree of Life. Eve knew of these things, too, but being tempted of the devil she was deceived and partook of the Tree of Knowledge anyway. She offered the fruit to Adam and he ate of it as well. Adam was not deceived, but he partook of the forbidden fruit because of being tempted with understanding and knowledge like God. Immediately the very life and presence of God departed out of their spirits and they began to live by their souls... no longer living by the consciousness of God within their spirits.

If Adam had partaken of the Tree of Life rather than the Tree of Knowledge, the divine life flow of God would have remained in mankind and sin would not have become the curse. But, because of Adam's disobedience, the Old Testament story of man is one of God's dealing and judgment through the law as He worked to bring man into obedience to what He had spoken.

Man in the Old Testament had a fallen nature that could not be inhabited by God without the miracle of Calvary and the resurrection.

But God had a plan—He would reinvade man's spirit and bring back to him what Adam had lost which is the real in-depth story of the birth of the new kingdom.

When Jesus was born of Mary into this world, the life stream in Him was not the life stream of an earthly father; it was the life stream of the heavenly Father. God was bringing His life back into humanity which the law had been governing up until that point. The law was given because of sin, but it could not keep man in line. God said that the law would remain until the seed (Jesus) would come. If the law could have given life, there would not have been any need for a new seed. There had to be a new and living way.

You and I are called to be sons of God because we have the same life in us that was in Jesus, the Son of God. If there are any women who struggle with being called a son of God, remember there are some men who feel funny about being called the bride of Christ. These words do not denote gender, they express the depth of the relationship.

AN EXCHANGED LIFE

No matter how you dress up the old, carnal nature of a man, get it to sing Gospel songs, slick down its cowlick and put a nice suit on it... that carnal nature that we were born with can never enter heaven. There has to be a new seed of life, a new nature implanted into our spirits. Christianity is an exchanged life, it is not an improvement on our old life—it is the beginning of a new life. This is a vitally important truth that too many of our churches and ministers do not teach. Your old nature is wicked and unredeemable; it must be totally exchanged in full for a new nature that is indwelt with the incorruptible seed of Jesus Christ.

There has to be a new and living way, a new kingdom that is not ruled by man or influenced by this world. This new kingdom and authority has to be absolutely dominant over all the forces of death and the enemy. The kingdom of God is everywhere; but the greatest deficit to His kingdom is those of us who fail to go far enough, soon enough, so that God can continue to expand and increase His kingdom. He is taking care of that, however, for He is increasing His people in spite of themselves.

The kingdom of God is like a treasure hid, a pearl of great price, that you need to press in to find. If you settle down on the edge of the kingdom of God, just inside the city limits, you will soon be disillusioned and may fall away.

Picture yourself going to Washington, D.C. You get to the sign that says, "Washington D.C., City Limits," and there you stop and set yourself down. You have arrived; you're inside of Washington, D.C. Can you imagine seeing all the wonders and the riches of that city from the edge of the city limits? You wouldn't see the White House, you wouldn't see the Library of Congress, you wouldn't see the Washington Monument, you would never experience the entire rich heritage of our country that has been restored and preserved there. You have to go all the way inside its very heart to see the fullness of a city.

Christianity cannot be treated like a step inside the city limits of the kingdom of God. You must go deeper and deeper into the heart of the kingdom of God, utterly abandoning yourself to the complete plans of God. When you go far enough in, you no longer hear the noise coming from the world outside as you follow the Holy Spirit from one magnificent experience to another on a tour of the kingdom that never ends. It is one glorious truth leading to another, one glorious revelation leading to another.

THE NEW KINGDOM FORETOLD

1 Peter 2:4-5 says, "As newborn babes (in Christ), desire the sincere milk of the word, that ye may grow thereby. If so be, ye have tasted that the Lord is gracious. To whom coming, as unto a living stone, disallowed indeed of men, but chosen of God, and precious. Ye also, as lively stones, are built up a spiritual house, a holy priesthood, to offer up spiritual sacrifices, acceptable to God by Jesus Christ." Jesus is the living stone that shall increase but you and I are the lively stones.

The world has rejected or disallowed the living stone, the chosen One of God, but that doesn't matter... Jesus is still the cornerstone. He is the cornerstone of society, of medicine, of education, of politics, of government and of all life. Yet the world does not know what to do with this rock of offence, the living stone Jesus. Israel does not know what to do with the living stone, nor do many of the other countries of the world. But, "Ye also, are lively stones... a spiritual house... a holy priesthood." Verse 9 says, "Ye are a chosen generation"... chosen from out of this world to be a royal priesthood.

We are a holy nation. There are three forces in the world today—Israel, the Gentiles and the Church. The church is composed of those who are born again out of the Jews and the Gentiles in this period of the Church age. We are the holy nation, a spiritual building made up of lively stones resting securely upon the cornerstone of Christ.

We are a chosen generation. Matthew 1:17 says, "So all the generations from Abraham to David are fourteen generations; and from David until the carrying away into Babylon are fourteen generations; and from the carrying away into Babylon unto Christ are fourteen generations." And there the genealogy stops. It says here that there are forty-two generations from Abraham to Christ. This was in the natural, physical realm.

It is here that Christ invades the death pattern of the generations from the fall of Adam right on through to the birth of Christ. Instead of another generation coming out of the loins of Christ as a man who was cut off to become the sacrifice for all mankind, He becomes the divine incorruptible seed. This seed comes out of the perfect life that Jesus lived and, through the miracle of His death and resurrection and the administrative work of the Holy Spirit, that seed is planted into the spirits of every man and woman who will receive it.

Matthew 1:18 begins; "Now the birth of Jesus Christ was on this wise..." This brings in the miracle birth of Christ. Out of Christ are all the generations that would follow that switch from the natural to the spiritual, opening up the new and living way so that every man and woman who will accept Christ can become a part of the generation that has a new nature.

The natural laws of human heredity do not have any effect with regard to this new nature. Because you are born again with a new nature in Christ, your children will not be born with that same nature. They must individually and personally come to Christ, who is the foundation of our faith and the life giver Himself, in order that they might become a part of this chosen generation as spoken by Peter.

Isaiah 53:8 declares, "He was taken from prison and from judgment; and who shall declare his generation? For he was cut off out of the land of the living; for the transgression of my people was he stricken." Jesus was cut off from the living without a lineage. He was not to sire any physical children and the natural generations ceased when it came to Him.

Jesus was cut off from the land of living without ever marrying to sire children in order to become a sacrifice for Israel and for the Gentiles. Yet He was to bring forth a new generation, a generation that had never before existed, a generation of spiritual children. He became the seed of that generation when He was nailed to the cross.

When you read the remarkable chapter of Isaiah 53 with its unlimited truth, there is one passage that I want you to particularly study, the latter part of verse 10 on through verse 11, "...he shall see his seed, he shall prolong his days, and the pleasure of the Lord shall prosper in his hand. He shall see of the travail of his soul, and shall be satisfied: by his knowledge shall my righteous servant justify many; for he shall bear their iniquities." Now, let us look at some prophecies in Psalms.

The prophecy of Psalm 22:30-31 says, "A seed shall serve him; it shall be accounted to the Lord for a generation. They shall come, and shall declare his righteousness unto a people that shall be born, that he hath done this."

Psalm 102:18 records this prophecy, "This shall be written for the generation to come; and the people which shall be created shall praise the Lord." Notice the word created. God had two sons, His only begotten Son, Jesus, and His recreated son, which we are.

In Psalm 102:28, "Thy children of thy servants shall continue, and their seed shall be established before thee." We can follow these truths right on through the entire Bible and find the never-ending story of the new kingdom, the chosen generation, which has come into being from these very prophecies.

Jesus' incorruptible seed was the seed that would create His offspring, His spiritual children. The "genetic" makeup or structure of that spiritual seed was completely tried and tested and found perfect. He had faced every sorrow and every tear and every trial and every temptation that you and I will ever face. He had the power of choice to fall as Adam did or to become the second Adam without sin. He was willing to forsake everything because He had you and me in mind. He passed that test and when He walked out of that tomb on resurrection morning, a new kingdom was birthed.

The Word of God was the seed or the spiritual sperm that birthed that new generation. "In the beginning was the Word, and the Word was with God, and the Word was God. The same was in the beginning with God. All things were made by him; and without him was not anything made that was made. In him was life; and the life was the light of men" (John 1:1-4). Jesus is the living and the written Word of God.

The soil prepared to receive His incorruptible seed is the human heart. The Holy Spirit quickens both the soil and the seed and a divine nature springs forth from the implanting. The miracle of spiritual birth occurs and a new creation in Christ is created.

THE GREAT TRANSITION

Jesus told His disciples that a woman in labour of childbirth travails and has sorrow because her hour is come, but as soon as she is delivered of the child, she remembers no more the anguish for the joy that her child is born into the world. He was trying to prepare them for His leaving. He was teaching that a great transition was about to occur... the Christ without who had walked on earth with them was about to go to the cross and die and be resurrected to become the spiritual Christ within them. Never again would they have to wonder where He was or why He hadn't yet joined them at a certain spot... for He was now to be inside of them wherever they went. The Christ without would now be the Christ within.

When you try to explain this new kingdom, this new generation, to those who only know Jesus as an example to try and pattern their lives after, they do not understand. Their spiritual walk is a dreary walk of failures and burdensome guilt. The man or woman who does not have the incorruptible seed of life within their spirits lives under condemnation.

None of us can keep the Ten Commandments or the Sermon on the Mount with our old nature. We cannot keep the law with our old nature. In order to be overcomers, we must have the new nature born in our spirits by the incorruptible seed of Christ. These old natures of ours are strong, resistant to change and covered with the power of sin. It takes the blood of Jesus Christ administered by the Holy Spirit to get inside of the innermost depths of our being to cleanse away the filth of yesterday and to open the door for His presence.

His indwelling presence is sufficient to end backsliding, depression, doubts, fear and torment. It is sufficient to lift us out of the ordinary and into the supernatural. This presence can bring so much "frontsliding" that we will never have time to backslide. Jesus has provided by His power everything necessary for our life and godliness (2 Peter 1:3). The only question is whether we will go far enough to lay hold of everything.

GREATER WORKS SHALL YE DO

That same Jesus who walked upon the water and healed the lepers and made the blind to see is still healing today. He is still healing the sick and feeding the poor and delivering the oppressed. He is still breaking open prison doors and setting the captives free. He is still doing miracles. In Acts 1:1, Luke said that he had given account of all that Jesus "began" both to do and teach. Jesus is still doing and teaching today and He is doing it through those of us who will allow Him to use us.

We must get the vision of what the Holy Spirit wants to do in each one of us if we will only let Jesus have complete control of our lives. Each Christian has the potential power within them, <u>held back only by their own limited vision and belief</u>, to kick over all the strongholds of "impossible" circumstances with every bondage, hindrance and struggle that comes with them. We have the power within us to march straight into the devil's territory and smash and destroy everything he has raised up against us and the work of God.

That same Spirit that raised Jesus from the dead now dwells within you and me. We are now standing on the very threshold of the Holy Spirit's unleashing of God's power and authority as never before through this last generation before the culmination of God's purposes. It is up to you and me as to whether or not we will be an active part of this glorious consummation of God's will for mankind.

CHAPTER 3

BRIDGING OUR GENERATION'S GAP

"Now learn a parable of the fig tree. When his branch is yet tender, and putteth forth leaves, ye know that summer is nigh. So likewise ye, when ye shall see all these things, know that it is near, even at the doors. Verily I say unto you; this generation shall not pass, till all these things be fulfilled. Heaven and earth shall pass away, but my words shall not pass away. But of that day and hour knoweth no man, no, not the angels of heaven, but my Father only. But as the days of Noah were, so shall also the coming of the Son of man be. For as in the days that were before the flood they were eating and drinking, marrying and giving in marriage, until the day that Noah entered into the ark. And knew not until the flood came, and took them all away; so shall also the coming of the Son of man be. Then two shall be in the field; the one shall be taken, and the other left. Two women shall be grinding at the mill; the one shall be taken, and the other left. Watch therefore; for ye know not what hour your Lord doth come. But know this, that if the goodman of the house had known in what watch the thief would come, he would have watched, and would not have suffered his house to be broken up. Therefore be ye also ready; for in such an hour as ye think not the Son of man cometh" (Matthew 24:32-44). "Truly, I tell you, this generation—that is, the whole multitude of people living at the same time, in a definite, given period—will not pass away till all these things taken together take place... But understand this: had the householder known in what [part of the night, whether in a night or a morning] watch the thief was coming, he would have watched and would not have allowed his house to be undermined and broken into" (Matthew 24:34,43, AMP).

This portion of Scripture is dealing with the part of this generation who are those in the household of faith living in this present hour. If you, the householder, are ready and know what is going on in the night or the day, then you will not let your household be undermined and broken through.

The world has been carefully structured by Satan to try to rob this generation of its faith, its virtue, its morals, and its uprightness so that it will slip into uncleanness, immorality and rebellion. This is the godless age that is spoken of in the Scriptures as how the last days shall be. It is a serious age, full of testing. This generation will see the beginnings of sorrows, "For nation shall rise against nation, and kingdom against kingdom... and there shall be famines and troubles; these are the beginnings of sorrows" (Mark 13:8). This is a generation that will know pressure and heartbreak.

YES, THIS REALLY IS THE LAST GENERATION

The Scriptures show clearly that this generation will not pass away until all these things are fulfilled. In 2 Timothy 3, it is not hard to see that the "perilous times" of the last days have truly arrived as we see the sins of man's nature so blatantly opposing God's Word today. The apostasy spoken of in 2 Thessalonians 2 and the mysteries of iniquity are at work like never before. The increased knowledge spoken of in Daniel 12 is now obvious in the rapidly developing technologies that are astounding the world. We can also see the regressive forces that have strived to hinder the results of all of the Gospel that has been taught, with so little of the signs and wonders of the early Church in evidence today.

The latest reports in today's newspapers, news magazines and other periodicals state that this is the largest generation that has ever been on earth. They also state that it has doubled in number in the past few years and will probably double itself again within the next few years to come. The youth population has increased tremendously with the greatest percentage of the people in some countries now being under twenty-five years of age. In today's world, particularly through the news media, tremendous advertising campaigns are being developed to reach the material desires of this generation. Not only are the youth being targeted, but every strata of society (including an increasing number of senior citizens) is being saturated through television, radio, music and entertainment to develop powerful materialistic desires which unfortunately are the backbone and strength of today's economy.

The minds behind education have an objective to plant a new god within the minds and spirits of all youth, called the god of the new age, which is built around secular humanism and materialism. The focus will be to satisfy the appetites of the fallen nature and indoctrinate them in concepts that are foreign to the Word of God. This alienation process is infiltrating our education systems so thoroughly that we can see the fruits of it in the behaviour of young adults everywhere as they are being encouraged to embrace these philosophies.

METALLIC PAINT AND GROUND GLASS

More young people today believe fiction to be truth than any other generation in history. This generation has been beguiled through false values packaged by the enemy in shiny glitter all pretty and bright, but in truth the shininess is nothing but harsh metallic paint and the glitter is ground glass. There is an underlying falseness in nearly everything that is being projected upon mankind by the systems of the world today.

God has His own way of wiping away the lies and purging the falseness of the world from people. All He has to do is let trouble and crisis come and men and women will find out very quickly how much the falseness and the fiction of the world's answers will help them in their hours of sorrow, pressure, reversals and even death. Fiction, masquerading as the patterns of truth, has brought iniquity into every area of life where there has not been the consistent purging and washing of the Word of God. It has even bent down the heads and the shoulders of many of God's people until they can no longer stand up under the stress of this age we live in because they have allowed themselves to be deceived.

This is an informed generation, one with more knowledge than any generation in the past. We know far more than our ancestors as the secrets of science and technology are now being rapidly unlocked. This is an educated generation living mainly in the cities of the nations. It is a generation that travels easily and quickly, shrinking the world in size.

Yet, with all these things, this remains one of the most ignorant generations ever with regard to truth and reality.

This generation is wise in material and secular knowledge and in the intricacies of the human mind with its drives and desires that motivate the carnal nature. It is a generation that has explored every form of self-gratification to the fullest until it is destroying itself; but it is a spiritually ignorant generation.

BORN WITH A SPIRITUAL CRY FOR GOD

We were born with a cry for God, but with a fallen nature that was in rebellion to God. Adam was born with something precious and sacred that he lost by sin and, for thousands of years, mankind has tried everything to satisfy the deep inner cry of that loss. Throughout the generations, men and women have tried the water holes of war, lust, greed, power, fame and popularity. But they are wells without water, clouds without rain. The whole world is still searching and knocking at every door. The mystery of the iniquity has sold mankind a bill of goods and none of the fountains of the world can produce the water of life that is needed.

We have churches on every corner, churches on television, churches that you can drive through and religious books and tapes everywhere. We have religious doctrines and beliefs and practices and movements all around us. Unfortunately, however, much of the church world today is apathetic and half asleep. Many great churches have lost touch with what is going on, they cannot tell the time or the season anymore. Too many Christians hear the truth and say, "I've been hearing that all my life, but nothing ever changes." What they do not realize is that they are changing; they are becoming more and more deceived as the enemy encroaches further upon their life every day.

Every moral concept from the teachings of the Bible is under fire today. Every principle of righteousness is being torn down all around us while we watch. Much of it is being destroyed right in our own living rooms on television as perversion and immorality are being presented as clever and smart. Adultery is being portrayed as sophisticated. Through television, children are being seduced by spirits into desires far beyond their age of comprehension.

PERILOUS TIMES HAVE COME

"But understand this, that in the last days there will set in perilous times of great stress and trouble—hard to deal with and hard to bear. For people will be lovers of self and [utterly] self-centered, lovers of money and aroused by an inordinate (greedy) desire for wealth, proud and arrogant and contemptuous boasters. They will be abusive (blasphemous, scoffers), disobedient to parents, ungrateful, unholy and profane. [They will be] without natural (human) affection (callous and inhuman), relentless–admitting of no truce or appeasement. [They will be] slanderers–false accusers, trouble makers; intemperate and loose in morals and conduct, uncontrolled and fierce, haters of good. [They will be] treacherous (betrayers), rash [and] inflated with self-conceit. [They will be] lovers of sensual pleasures and vain amusements more than and rather than lovers of God" (2 Timothy 3:1-4 AMP).

This is the end result of the feeding of the self-life that fights for mastery within every one of us. Two masters cannot rule your life or your house, only one can and that one master will either be Christ or self. The more that you die to the carnal desires and the motivations of self, the more Christ can live and grow within you. The more that you feed your self-life upon the things of the world, the more your spiritual life is pushed back into a corner. Have you ever seen a plant or a young tree that is crowded into a dark corner behind several other fast growing plants or trees? It becomes spindly, weak and stunted in growth, eventually leading to the death of the plant that was once full of life and promise.

This is the day of the rule of the self-life... the day of doing your own thing. "Have it your own way... you deserve a break... you owe it to yourself... it costs more, but you're worth it... you only go around once, so grab all you can get!" Have you really listened to what television is programming into the minds of people?

Unfortunately, many of our churches today are also feeding the self-life of the carnal man and not feeding the spiritual man. People want to be entertained, they want to be comforted, they want to be blessed and they want to be reassured that everything is fine. They want their altars padded and their pews soft. They want to have their emotions satisfied, but they don't want to be made uncomfortable in their level of spiritual maturity. They want "fast food spiritual feeding" and "convenience Christianity."

This type of Christianity will never be able to hold up under the stress and the pressures of these days. This is why many backslide when the hard times hit, because they have no real depth of faith or spiritual understanding to draw upon. Much of this unsaved generation is headed straight for hell because God-professing people have not gone far enough to take hold of the fullness of God in this age in which we live.

PRAYING THROUGH

God is sufficient for this age, but God must also have a people who are sufficient. He needs a people who have gone far enough to have the fires of the altar burning within their souls. We need to get down on our knees and stay there until things begin to surge and swell within our hearts and the glory starts coming through, until our desires and our purposes are renewed. This takes time, dedication, energy and effort. We are not going to carry our unsaved loved ones and our rebellious children into heaven with us if we are only willing to invest a few minutes of prayer here and there for their future.

The time for babying ourselves and making excuses is over. There are responsibilities upon our shoulders that must be prayed through until victory comes. If we procrastinate and do not enter in to lay hold of the provisions God has for us, then the responsibility for problems and failures in every aspect of our lives will lay squarely at our own door. Our heartaches and disappointments cannot be laid at the doorway of the promises of God.

Men and women will tragically stagger under ever increasing burdens in the days to come because of their unwillingness to press into victory.

There is an old phrase that is used among many Christians, the phrase of "praying through." This does not mean a lot to some, but to others it is spelled SUCCESS. God has provided answers in His Word and faith is developed through His Word. The key is to enter into the Word and prayer until the truth of God is made real within your spirit. Hebrews 11 records many miraculous things which took place by faith in the lives of men and women of prayer. As we make His promises and His answers ours through faith, the reality of answered prayer begins to come forth within our own life.

As we pray and lay hold of God, we begin to sense that holy life of Christ surging through our soul and spirit as God intended. We must not let our old self-nature crawl off the altar that it is being sacrificed upon until we have prayed through to a victory that is sensed in our spirit by faith. Once we sense the victory in our spirit, it doesn't matter what the circumstances look like in the natural... the victory is there! We have prayed through.

This is the day when we all want to use substitutes and we want to take the easy way, but the easy way is only a temporary relief. The "easy way" will never provide the answers that can bring real change in the midst of our circumstances. Praying through, the hard way, is what brings the answers to the cry of our hearts, for we will never see our families saved or touch the world with a haphazard pattern of prayer and spiritual warfare.

Set your mind on getting rid of your "but, but" religion. "I know I should pray more, but... I really should have stopped and witnessed to her, but... The Lord knows I'd work with those teenagers if I could, but..." All of those buts are really nothing but a rebellious heart whether you want to think so or not.

You were made for God; you were not made for the world. It is the devil's work to so entrap us in time schedules and so many "important" things that we lose sight of the real things that matter, the things of God. Jesus is not going to take a bride for Himself who is half-filled and half-hearted, one who has been coasting along on her denomination's beliefs and her pastor's religion. Jesus is going to take Himself a bride who is filled to overflowing with the Spirit of God, cleansed and made holy without spot or blemish, and brimming over with love in her heart.

Never lose your love for prayer and for the study of the Word of God. Those are the sources of the power in your spiritual warfare and the consistency in your witnessing and discipling of others.

A NEW DAY DAWNING

God is dong a new thing today, something very unique and special. He is dealing very specifically with His people as individuals. Gone are the days when you could bask in the blessings and the glories of the outpouring of the Holy Spirit in your church as a corporate body. There is a new outpouring of the Spirit to meet an intensified hunger to know Him personally. The churches will still be here and be blessed and see the glories of the Lord, but those individuals who want to move to the next level with God will press far beyond just listening to their pastor on Sunday. These are the Christians who will never settle for spiritual fast food or convenience Christianity, these are the ones who are determined to be ready and not be caught short such as the five foolish virgins who had not prepared themselves. These are the Christians who will be as close to Jesus as they know how to get, they will be crying out in their spirits in unity with the Holy Spirit, "Come, Lord Jesus, come... I've been waiting for you!"

THE PROCESS OF PERFECTING

This is the "X" generation, the redeemed generation that will give birth to the coming of the Son of God. The wickedness that is rampant within the present generation of godless men and women is the very thing that is going to perfect righteousness of this redeemed generation of Christians. God will allow the world to test every area of your life. You will know where you need more consecration and you will become stronger as you press forward in your prayers to attain it. When something hits an area that makes you flinch or cry out, "Don't touch that, that's mine," then you know that is where you'd better start.

We must be wise to the hour in which we live. This means we have to go far enough in our Christian experience that Christ is so revealed in each one of us that we can meet the challenge of the increasing darkness that is all about us.

God will honour your reaching out for more of Him and He will reveal His Son in you until you walk calmly upon the troubled waters of this world. The sufficiency of Christ will so guide and move your life that your glow of radiance will be apparent to all.

If you don't go far enough, you will be defeated by the darkness and the iniquity of these times. There won't be any fence sitters as we move into these final days; no one will be straddling the line anymore. You will either be in or you will be out. If you are not all the way in, then you need another encounter with God.

FOUR WAYS TO BUILD THE SPIRITUAL BRIDGE

Can the gap from one side of this generation to the other be bridged? The success of doing this is not going to be found with the psychologists, psychiatrists, programs, education, training or how-to books. It will not be found in documentaries, talk shows or "meaningful" dialogue with the humanists. We must understand that the basic problem of our day is spiritual.

There is, however, something that no one in this generation can resist and that is the power of God burning and working through us as believers. The first one of the four things that can build the bridge to span this gap in our generation, the final pursued generation, is that our religious doctrine must be changed into an actual spiritual experience. We must be able to present the proof of an encounter with the power of God.

The second part of the bridge is a clear, uncompromising testimony backed up by a life that lines up with it in every way. I remember one young person saying, "I don't understand what you're saying, but your life is screaming at me." Seeing a sermon lived out in a life is twenty times more powerful than hearing a sermon any day.

The third part of the bridge is a willingness to accept responsibility and put it into action. There are many churches and fellowships today without pastors and there are thousands of Sunday school classes that have no teachers because people do not want to carry the responsibility.

This is a complicated world in which we live today. If we fail here, we are offering our loved ones and our children up to the gods of this world because we have allowed <u>our lives</u> to become so complicated that we do not have the time or the energy to touch <u>their lives</u> for eternity.

The fourth and final piece of the bridge and the ultimate wisdom in reaching this generation is that you have to love... really love. Not just saying the words, but you must love to the point that you are willing to do something that costs you. You're willing to pray, you're willing to go the extra mile, you're willing to give, you're willing to help in Sunday School, you're willing to open your home for a Bible study, you're willing to do whatever God asks you to do.

You know how easy it is to love the child who is doing exactly what he or she should be doing, the kid who does everything just right. We have to remember that people, young or old, who have not been raised on the "things" of God, also need love. Those people who are mean, hostile, rebellious, unloving and rough-edged. You can never reach them without love. Those who have sinned need love; those who have failed need love. Those who are just plain miserable to be around need love. The Church is not supposed to be a rest home; it is a hospital! Jesus is the doctor, we are the medical assistants, the prayer rooms are the operating rooms and the altars are the emergency rooms.

We can bridge the gap, but we won't bridge it with programs or entertainment or sensational speakers. We'll bridge it by the power of God surging through our lives to touch those around us and bring them into an encounter with the only power that will meet the hunger of this age, Jesus Christ!

CHAPTER 4

PREPARING THIS GENERATION TO BIRTH THE RETURN OF CHRIST

The Scriptures of Revelation 22:16 and 17 are a penetrating passage which cover an unlimited depth of understanding of the eternal purpose and plan in the return of Christ. Verse 16 states, "I Jesus have sent mine angel to testify unto you these things in the churches. I am the root and the offspring of David, and the bright and morning star." Many teachings on prophecy try to place the book of Revelation from chapter four on through the end as being after the rapture of the Church. But here we see that Jesus is saying that He has sent an angel to testify of the things that were written in the churches, which means the Church is still here and the rapture has not taken place. He was speaking to them of truths that would be as insights and guidelines for His coming again.

Verse 17 says, "And the Spirit and the bride says, Come..." He is dealing here with two distinct forces in His divine purpose:

1) "And the Spirit..." deals with the administrator of everything that Jesus accomplished through His death and resurrection, the Holy Spirit. It is the Spirit who will fulfill Christ's purpose in coming to this world to prepare a bride for Himself. It is the Holy Spirit who is now moving in this final dispensation to deal with, convince and convict the men and women of this

generation who are Christians to be prepared to speak the same language that the Spirit is speaking.

2) The second force is the bride, the redeemed who are the overcomers. When the bride and the Spirit begin to speak the same language, when the bride is in that level of relationship of complete surrender and maturity, then Jesus can come again. The Spirit of God and the bride must be made as one before the climate is ready for Jesus' return. The last part of verse 17 says, "...And let him that heareth say, come. And let him that is athirst come. And whosoever will, let him take the water of life freely."

Again, it is the one language of the Spirit and the bride speaking together in unity saying, "Come," that will bring the return of our Lord Jesus Christ.

God made the earth for His children and then He separated it from eternity and called it into the framework of time. But time has to have an end as it says in Revelation 10:6, "...there should be time no longer," when eternity will take over again. As this final happening approaches, there will be that one last generation at the end of time as we know it. We are that generation, the privileged people that the prophecies of thousands of years have been focused upon. God has waited for this generation since the beginning of time. This is the hour that He began to look forward to some six thousand years ago.

When Adam needed a companion, God created woman for him out of his side. Angels couldn't fulfill that position; it took another human who was made in the likeness and image of God. When Jesus needed a companion, His bride, He went to the cross to experience death and resurrection. Then, out of His side, came a life that would be implanted into men and women all over the world... men and women who had been born spiritually dead to God, but who were now spiritually alive unto Christ. These redeemed men and women would make up His bride, His companion, for all eternity.

The prophets envisioned it and foretold of it in the Old Testament. The disciples foretold of it in their day and longed to be a part of it. But this is the generation that is going to see and experience the actual culmination of God's purposes for mankind. We already are and will experience even more of the unusual as we sense the new dimensions of God's power and presence in the world today. There will be movings of the Spirit of God that you and I have only been able to wonder at and try to understand in the Scriptures. Our forefathers laboured, suffered, wept and even died for this hour. They knew that there was coming a time, if they were faithful, when either they or their seed would finally see that which God had promised come to pass.

A WORLD IS CRYING!

All over this world there are people who love Jesus and who are reaching out for something more than they have ever known before. There is something in the very atmosphere of this world at this time that we cannot put our finger upon. Something elusive is moving, breathing and growing in the spirit world. It is the final coming together of the Father's plan. The nations of the world are but a checkerboard to God as He moves the pieces towards the end of the game. If you have any doubt as to who is going to win the game, just read the last page of the story (the Bible). God's people win!

We are actually living in this incredible final age. It is hard to realize that the greatest percentage of the largest generation ever to live at one time on this earth has no idea that the end of time is about to happen. The world and unfortunately even much of the Church does not comprehend what is now taking place. If they did, they would not be involved in the trivial, temporal pursuits and things of the world; they would be working feverishly for what will count in eternity.

There is an unusual depth of hunger that God has placed within this generation. Some have pursued this hunger to its source and found a relationship with God. Millions of others have pursued it down every empty avenue the world offers and their unmet need has only intensified, driving them to speed up their search. This lack of spiritual fulfillment is the force that drives souls into alcohol and drugs; into immorality and perversion; into the quest for power, possessions and empires... this is the force that ultimately leads to destruction and death if it is not channelled towards God.

The dictionary describes hunger as a craving, an urgent need, an eager or strong desire, a yearning or a longing for something. It is a powerful physical, emotional and spiritual reaction of the body to a need. God intended that this hunger would bring His people to Him, their greatest source. Tragically, many have searched the ways of sin to try to quench the hunger. Habitual sin has an accumulative effect upon the person who will not turn and allow God to cleanse them of its terrible, ever-increasing burden. This state of bondage will dull their spiritual senses and inflame their physical senses, further blinding them to the real source of the hunger. The urgent hunger is felt and the physical senses override the spirit's cry and demand release from the power of the need.

Blessed are those who have fine tuned their spiritual senses through prayer and communion with the Father and who have crucified their physical senses, dying daily to "self." Their first reaction to that hunger deep within their spirit is to drop to their knees in prayer or to immerse themselves in the Word of God.

As Christians, we are our brother's keeper… whether it is the brother and sister across the backyard fence or in the country across the ocean. We are responsible for the man and woman whose hand we have never taken, whose eyes we have yet to look into. We have a responsibility as this generation, the pursued generation, to bring Jesus to those at our work, in our neighbourhood, on the street and around the world.

Many people living in torment and fear in the world today have been to church, but they didn't find Jesus—they found religion. Enough "religion" can make you immune to the Gospel, but the Church is going to be loosed from being tongue-tied, from being intimidated and from being "religious." Christians are going to be stepping out, boldly proclaiming the promises of God—walking the streets to reach the unreached with Jesus walking inside of them. You, as a child of God, are going to discover who you really are and you will no longer get your conduct and your identity mixed up.

We all naturally have some timidity in us; we don't want to be foolish or make a spectacle of ourselves, but we do want to be used of God. In order to do this, we must not fear stepping out. Every supernatural miracle of God is preceded by an act of the will. We must be willing to respond to the flesh's question of, "What if I fail?" with the answer of, "So what? More of my ego and self will melt away if I do."

ARE YOUR SHOES TOO SMALL?

The Holy Spirit has been fairly quiet for a number of years but He is now pulling down strongholds and the walls of differences between God's people. He is bringing the different denominations into a common understanding. This generation that is being pursued by God is going to speak as one in unity with the Holy Spirit.

Too many churches have stopped and camped on truths that God revealed to them. This is what has created separate doctrines and the different denominations that have led to strife and division within the body of Christ. It is easier to build a doctrine upon one truth than to experience the cost and the growing pains of moving further on into deeper truths. The revelation of Christ in the Word is a progressive thing. What we think we know today is only the seed of something greater that God wants to reveal to us tomorrow. The Word is <u>unlimited</u> in it possibilities and potential—it is meant to be used like building blocks—line upon line, precept upon precept—in our spiritual growth and progressive revelation.

Do you remember when you got a new pair of shoes when you were younger and, for purposes of anticipated growth, your mother usually purchased them too large for you. But you loved them and wore them proudly. This is like the truth of God—some truths are a little too large for you when you first try them on (this is to give you room to grow in the new truth you have just received), but you joyfully walk in these new truths anyway because you know that they are yours to claim and to use. Then you began to grow into those shoes and the day came when they started to pinch and get too small. You needed a larger pair of shoes to accommodate your growing feet.

The Word of God is progressive and you must always be prepared to try on new levels of understanding of God's truths that will fit the size of your spiritual maturity—new truths that you have grown into. One example is that when you were first born again, you could understand that Jesus died on the cross for you. If you were given a deeper understanding at that point that you, too, were going to have to put your "flesh" on the cross and crucify it, it would be an element of the truth of the crucified life that you might never have been able to handle as a brand new Christian. A baby Christian can understand and handle love and forgiveness. Only a more mature Christian who has moved on in new levels of understanding of God's truths can understand and handle dying to self, forgiving others unconditionally and the walk of faith in the midst of great testing.

You constantly need to allow the Word of God to enlarge that inner part of Christ's life within you. You may not always feel good as He does this; growing pains can really hurt as certain areas begin to press against other areas, forcing them to expand whether they are ready to or not. That is when you pray for God to enlarge your capacity for the revelation of Christ within you.

The progressive revelation of the Word of God is why the Bible never gets old, regardless of how many times you may read it in a hundred years. This is why Christianity never grows stale unless you deliberately allow it to become stale through neglect.

LAYING HOLD OF ETERNAL LIFE

Take a moment to picture the Apostle Paul in your mind. See him as the Christian who had been shipwrecked, beaten with rods, stoned, criticized by his brethren, wounded in spirit and in body by those who professed the name of Jesus as well as by those who were unsaved. What did he say to all of this? He cried out, "Who shall separate us from the love of Christ? Shall tribulation, or distress, or persecution, or famine, or nakedness, or peril, or sword... Nay, in all things we are more than conquerors through him that loved us" (Romans 8:35, 37). He knew that the Anointed One was within him and that nothing could separate him from Jesus.

Paul was held prisoner in a miserable, filthy Roman jail with only a small opening at the top of his cell through which his captors would drop his food. The stench and filth of the bodily excretions all around him caused many to die. Chained to a stone with only the flickering light of a candle, he wrote to the Church in Philippi passionately saying, "That I might know him..." (Philippians 3:10). This was the Paul who had "known" Christ for twenty-eight years since his encounter with Him on the Damascus Road. Yet he was seeking still a further revelation of Christ to know him better, because Paul understood that to know Christ was an ongoing, progressive revelation of that most magnificent, divine life of the ages.

As he was chained there, Paul exhorted the Philippians over and over to "Rejoice!" Here he was chained to a stone in the most hideous, smelly situation imaginable and he was rejoicing. Why? Because Paul knew he had the life of Jesus within him and that he was not limited to his physical body. Think of how you and I cry, "Unfair!" when someone says an unkind word about us. Think of how we wail when we run short of money and debts mount or when we smash our little finger or our body doesn't feel good. That is Adam's old nature coming up in you, but don't worry... the Holy Spirit is rooting him out of you.

REACHING FOR OUR NEW BODIES

Paul prayed for the Church in Galatia that Christ would be fully formed within them. He knew that Christ being revealed in them more and more would mean less room left in their flesh for the devil to work on. This ongoing process of a greater revelation of Christ within and a dying to the flesh without brings us closer and closer to our new bodies.

The Bible says, "(He) will change our vile body, that it may be fashioned like unto His glorious body, according to the working whereby he is able even to subdue all things unto himself" (Philippians 3:21). This generation is reaching for its new body. Those who are saved are reaching for their glorified body; those who are unsaved are reaching desperately for a body that simply can survive the pollution, chemicals, stress and diseases attacking on every side. We have more doctors, more hospitals, more medicine and more hospital plans than the world has ever known before because we have more sickness and disease than ever before.

As a nation, we take our vitamins, drink our juice, jog our bodies, exercise our muscles, eat our health foods and spend millions to keep these old carcasses of flesh maintained and in repair. We decorate them to the best of our ability. Only the Christian who has laid hold of the resurrection life of Jesus Christ has a life that is going uphill.

There is something unparalleled within the child of God that is building to a victorious climax. When Paul said, "But if the Spirit of him that raised up Jesus from the dead dwell in you, he that raised up Christ from the dead shall also quicken your mortal bodies by his Spirit that dwelleth in you" (Romans 8:11), he knew what he was talking about. The Christian has the inside track to triumphant living—spiritually, mentally, emotionally and physically. God has promised us something that is beyond the normal boundaries and limits of the natural world. When you lay hold of eternal life, I mean really lay hold of it, then He will do something inside of your body that will even slow your aging.

Do you want to know how to lay hold of the miracle of youthfulness and good health? Just get so busy for God and so active in His purposes and plans that He has to miraculously revitalize you in order to keep you going. The more valuable you are in helping to win the world for Jesus, the more attention He is going to pay to keeping you and your body running smoothly. Which race car gets the high powered new engine, the most attention, the fancy tune ups and the big tires? The one that is out with the leaders in the fast lane or the one that transports the pit crew to the parking lot? Think about it.

CRISES BRING SPIRITUAL BREAKTHROUGH

When God is moving you further into Himself, He usually allows a crisis to come into your life. Satan is constantly trying to pull you away from the center of the Gospel with pressure, sorrow, heartache and problems. I think it must be the ultimate frustration for him when God turns the very difficulty Satan intended for your downfall into a means to raise you to a higher level of faith and maturity. When God needs to get your attention or to move you to a higher spiritual plane, He will sometimes let things pass through your door that cause you to feel that the rug is being pulled out from under you.

Jesus tells the Holy Spirit to hound your footsteps, break up your sleep and put you in the pressure cooker if you aren't listening to Him. If it takes a crisis to get your attention, then God says, "Let there be crisis."

Keep your eyes on Him and know that as He brings you through each circumstance in your life, He is walking you on a path that will lead you to a higher level with Him than you were on before. You will be able to see more of the valley beneath you than you ever were able to see before. This is because you are further up the mountain with Him. It is only when we doubt and disbelieve and flail about in despair that the path through the circumstances will lead downward, back over previously gained territory that will have to be reclaimed again.

Many people don't like to hear that kind of thing, but if you're seeking Jesus with every fibre of your being, it is already too late. You love Him, He loves you and you need each other—you are partners in the work of redemption. The bride of Christ and the Holy Spirit must work together to bring forth that final harvest of our generation.

Jesus is only getting you ready to be a powerful warrior in the army of God; He is infusing you with hope and with courage. Through the circumstances in your life, He is breaking the cords inside you that have held you earthbound. Through each circumstance that comes into your life, He is just breaking the chains that have locked you into the thought patterns of the world. There is no need to fear or to live in torment as the world lives. Our body is a vehicle that is very important to God's divine purposes. We can say, "Jesus, you are alive in me, so I'm ready for anything."

Only the Christian who will go far enough with God will not have to worry about their motivation to continue on or the outcome of their future. When enough of Jesus Christ is revealed inside of you, you will know that your destiny is completely in God's control and you are going to live just exactly as long as the days of your usefulness are ordained. Then you will have the glorious privilege of going home, unless Jesus returns first. If some of you should go before the rapture, then you have just cheated on us. You just got ahead of the rest of us. Either way, once your days on earth are through... you're going to go into the presence of God!

There are many different opinions as to when Jesus is going to come back, before the tribulation or after the tribulation. Some say the Church is going to go through the tribulation. Don't argue with them; just let their faith be as it is. Just know one thing—when you have the life of the Son in you, God is not going to pour His wrath out upon the life of His Son. Because we are the body of His Son, God will take us out of here before He pours forth His wrath.

GOING HOME

In days past, a dear old saint graced our church with his presence. He was still teaching a Bible class at eighty-two years of age. I received a phone call from him one day, "Pastor, can you come over? Mama just went home to be with the Lord." I went over immediately and there he sat, praising the Lord, without a tear in his eye. He had said to the Lord, "God, you have taken her home. I'm going to miss her, but I'm glad she's home." We had prayer with him and then stayed until the family came and the final arrangements were made.

A short while later, he said to me, "Pastor, I'm not going to be here much longer. God has told me He is going to take me home." This dear old saint began fasting for a revival meeting we were going to have at the church. He was praying for our church to be a mighty vehicle of the Gospel to touch our city of Sacramento. He kept getting progressively weaker and weaker, but still he pressed in through prayer and fasting as he believed God had told him to do to lay hold of spiritual breakthroughs for this revival. Because of poisons building up in his system, he was finally taken to the hospital. It was then that he told me that God had said he would go home six months to the day after his beloved "Mama" had gone. At this time, it was only a few days away from being six months. He said, "I'm going home in a few days and I'm going to have a new body. I won't have to struggle with this one anymore."

On the final day of the sixth month, I stood by his bedside as he lay under an oxygen tent. He smiled at me and said, "The Pilot is coming now. Pastor, I won't see you anymore. Keep doing just what you're doing, keep preaching Jesus. It's just about over and I can hardly wait. Goodbye, Pastor."

Then I left his bedside to go to church for the Wednesday night prayer meeting.

Twenty minutes into the service, the phone buzzed softly on the platform. "Just to inform you, Brother Belcher just slipped away to be with the Lord." Right on schedule... just as the Holy Spirit had spoken to him. He was prepared and was reaching out for his new body.

It was when I was serving in my first pastorate in the state of Washington, entering into some of the greatest realities of a relationship in Jesus that I had ever known, that I received word that my mother was extremely ill. I traveled to Oakland, California, and stood beside the bed of this faithful soldier of Christ. She had been a nurse, often serving as the only source of medical help when there were no doctors in the communities she lived in. She had an unusual faith that she instilled in her children and, though I tried, I never could run away from the awareness of her faith in God and His presence in her life.

I remember once when a doctor pronounced a young teenager dead of double pneumonia and spinal meningitis as he lay in our local hospital. After the doctor had walked out, my mother went in and closed the door behind her. Later, after her faith and her prayers had touched heaven, she opened the door and walked out with the boy. This put something inside of me that I never could get away from in all my early years of running away from God.

But when the word came that my mother was ill and I went to be by her side as the oldest son, we were told she had a rare disease. The doctors did not know the cause or the cure. I prayed with her, sat by her side and read Scripture to her. Sitting by her bed, God gave me the message for Easter Sunday which was a week away, "WHY SEEK YE THE LIVING AMONG THE DEAD?"

I returned to my church on Easter Sunday and preached this message straight from my heart and from the reality that had broken forth in my understanding of the higher purposes of Jesus Christ within our lives. Tuesday morning the phone rang and my father said, "Mother has gone to be with the Lord."

This new reality had a strange effect on me. I couldn't cry, I couldn't sorrow and I couldn't grieve for my dear mother's departure from her earthly body. At the funeral I worried for fear people would think something was wrong with me; for though I had loved her as dearly as any son could, I wanted to run up and down the aisle crying out, "Why seek ye the living among the dead?"

Reality had broken in my spirit and death had lost its sting. Reality had broken down that barrier in my heart that can bring such torment to those who lose their loved ones. I have never returned to her grave and I have never placed flowers there. She isn't there and she never was. She had gone home to be with the Lord the minute she ceased her earthly breath. She was absent from her body, present with the Lord... she had graduated into the glorious presence of Jesus.

I pray that God will be able to instil such a faith and understanding of our future in each one of His children. This life on earth is only a dressing room for our lifetime in eternity, this is only the time of adorning... a time of building our character and strengthening our spirits. This is a time when Jesus is filling us with His attributes and His grace. We're all going to be together forever and that is a pretty long time. God has to use a little sandpaper on some of us right now, rubbing off our rough spots so that we will be able to spend eternity together.

UNDER CONSTRUCTION

A new spiritual man is being formed beneath the veil of flesh in each one of us right now. That familiar passage of Scripture so beautifully penned by the Apostle Paul says, "For we know that if our earthly house of this tabernacle were dissolved we have a building of God, an house not made with hands, eternal in the heavens. For in this we groan, earnestly desiring to be clothed upon with our house which is from heaven; if so be that being clothed, we shall not be found naked. For we that are in this tabernacle do groan, being burdened; not for that we would be unclothed, but clothed upon, that mortality might be swallowed up of life." (2 Corinthians 5:1-4).

We may not understand it or see it with our natural eyes, but inside of us, week in and week out, day in and day out, through the Word of God, through prayer, through nights of intercession, through worship—the power of God is at work inside of you and there is a new spiritual man in the making. The new man is not after the fashion of your fleshly body... this is a new inner spiritual man. His likeness and image is being formed and framed in you as Paul prayed for the Church of Galatia, that Christ would be fully formed within them. In fact, Jesus is speeding up the process and there is more spiritual "pressure per square inch" today than there was a few years ago. He is not going to let us coast up to the edge of eternity; He is pursuing you and directing you into a triumphant march towards your destiny.

CHAPTER 5

THE UNCTION OF THE HOLY ONE

Too often we settle for substitutes in our lives rather than what God wants to bring forth inside each one of us. We settle for just meeting together, giving our tithes and offerings and putting in our predetermined, daily allotment of time to read the Word and pray. Instead of just being willing to spend the accepted amount of time necessary in order to survive spiritually, each one of us should be heading straight into the eye of the very storm itself. We should be aggressively heading into human need, into breakthroughs in the spirit world and into reclaiming the very things that people have lost in God.

It is impossible to just maintain a status quo as a Christian. Satan will never let you and neither will the Holy Spirit. You must either move forwards in God or slide backwards in Satan, there is no standing still. As Christians, we must be on the move for there is an anointing from heaven—the unction of the Holy One—that must be carried forward to those in need. If you try to stand still with it, you will either lose it through carelessness or Satan will knock it from your hands.

This unction will bring miracles, heal sickness, dissolve burdens, mend broken hearts, heal marriages and restore families and relationships. But there is a price to be paid to participate in the ministry of this divine unction.

The religious "armchair philosopher" calling spiritual plays from the sidelines will never have it. No one will have it unless they get on their knees in faith, armed with a full knowledge of the Word that is strengthened daily through reading the Bible, and diligently seek God for it.

This is the divine plan and the power behind the Gospel. Jesus came to make us whole... spirit, soul and body. He is the One who bore the curse and set us free so that we could be truly whole through life in Him. All the blessings of the wonderful family name of Jesus Christ belong to the body of Christ. We need to be prepared to lay hold of them and to take them through the unction of God to those around us who do not understand this.

We are not part of this world; we are only enduring it as we are on our way home from earth to heaven. Every step that we move closer to Jesus and every time we press in until we receive the unction of the Holy Spirit, we have just cut another rope tied to the moorings of the earth and we are released to be a little freer from the limitations of our flesh.

As the unction of God heals the breaches that are between men and women in the body of Christ, we will become one Spirit, one body and one force moving upon the face of the earth to bring forth the manifestation of the Lord Jesus Christ. A true body of believers that knows how to move with the Spirit of God is the only answer to the dilemma of the world today and the aches of the human heart. The Scriptures speak of the unction as follows: "But you hold a sacred appointment, you have been given an unction. You have been anointed by the Holy One, and you all know the Truth" (1 John 2:20 AMP).

"But it is God Who confirms and makes us steadfast and establishes us (in joint fellowship) with you in Christ, and has consecrated and anointed us—enduing us with the gifts of the Holy Spirit. He has also appropriated and acknowledged us as His, putting His seal upon us and giving us His Holy Spirit in our hearts as the security deposit and guarantee of the fulfillment of His promise" (2 Corinthians 1:21-22 AMP).

Whenever you purchase something of such a magnitude that you must make payments on it, you seal your guarantee to purchase this item by making a "deposit" on it. This deposit thereby provides security that you will complete your half of the transaction. God has put His seal on us and placed His Holy Spirit in our hearts as a deposit and guarantee that He will fulfill His "transaction" with us to provide a place in eternity with Him as well as on earth here and now as His sons and daughters.

He has put His seal upon you by the Holy Spirit if you have accepted His salvation. The Spirit has been commissioned to be constantly with you wherever you go. If you seem to be having a lot of trouble in your life, perhaps you need to check your obedience to the Holy Spirit within you as He guides and checks your "goings."

THE PAINFUL PRICE OF PROGRESS

In the early part of 1986, there was much pain in the hearts and the spirits of the people of America caused by the price of progress in the space program. There were enormous sacrifices paid in the ongoing quest to gain knowledge about outer space and space travel. Seven astronauts disappeared in a fiery explosion that left all of America grieving and heartbroken.

With the tremendous discoveries and breakthroughs in technology, science and knowledge in America has also come the price of tragedy and loss. Many, many lives were lost as pioneers forged across America to open up new frontiers. A high cost has been paid for our expertise in new sources of transportation. The developing of new forms of energy has produced triumph and tragedy alike. The by-product of toxic wastes from our breakthroughs in producing powerful new chemicals is an ongoing source of heartbreak to mankind and the wild creatures of nature.

We live in two worlds; the natural world that we taste, touch, smell, see and hear every day, and the spiritual world. These two worlds parallel each other in certain ways. Whenever there are great strides forward in the natural world, we can expect an increase in the spirit world as well. But just as it takes sacrifice and pain to bring about breakthroughs in the natural world, it takes the same to bring about breakthroughs in the spirit world.

In any quest to conquer new territory in the spirit world, we know that there will be things to overcome. We must realize that in addition to the reactionary factors all around us, there are reactions that can take place within us as well when we move out into the unknown. These new frontiers are not foreign to God, His Word or to experienced believers who have already moved into them... but we are often entering into a new realm of spiritual warfare as we set out to take territory from the enemy.

There are several reactionary factors that can occur as we press in to bring forth spiritual breakthroughs. The first one is attitude. When difficulty of a long duration confronts us, it is very easy to develop a negative attitude unless we stay in right relationship with the One who gives the breakthroughs to us. We can be very human in our discouragement, reacting in ways that usually end in disobedience. We must remember that only through Christ will we constantly lay hold of the eternal life factors that bring consistent victory.

Another dangerous factor when stepping out on new spiritual ground is self-centeredness. The moment the unusual takes place in our quest for victory and God brings breakthroughs, we often try to relate it to ourself instead of realizing that we were only the channel or the vehicle through which God brought forth the answer. Man, throughout history, has often ruined, sidetracked or polluted the great moves of God's Holy Spirit which were manifested to meet the needs of humanity. Never lose sight of the fact that it was only through God that a victory or an answer came or you may find yourself out there batting spiritual warfare on your own self-merit. I wouldn't want to be in your shoes if that happened.

Another factor is carelessness. We are always up on our toes at the starting line, but once we get out ahead and successes come, it is easy to relax and become permissive with "the little foxes that spoil the grapes." It is in this careless environment that we often don't recognize the things of the enemy sneaking up on us to defeat us.

These are only a few of the inner reactions we may encounter in ourselves when we move out to break new ground in the spirit world. We must remember to keep our spiritual guard up, to constantly check our attitudes to see if they are lining up with the Word of God and to remain on our spiritual toes.

To be a consistent overcomer who is victorious in a world that needs the unusual from God, we must always be out on the cutting edge. History tells us of tremendous spiritual breakthroughs by the Spirit of God that have given birth to religious organizations, fresh dimensions in Christianity and new patterns of lifestyle for multitudes who have experienced the realities of the indwelling life of Christ. Then, in order to maintain those patterns and successes, doctrines and dogmas and rituals and regulations began to be established to protect the breakthroughs of yesterday.

Once we try to hold ourselves steady by the past, we enter into avenues of diminishing anointing because God is a progressive God. Truth is progressive, revelation is progressive.

Christian, you cannot stand still, either you progress or you regress. What was yesterday was good, but God wants to always build upon that which was and bring in new and greater manifestations that will challenge the developing spirits of men and women moving for Him.

As we continue to progress spiritually and we find ourselves confronting the concepts, patterns and successes of yesterday, we must never think of them as being absolute or God's final answer. Rather we should view them as being the steps to even greater manifestations of God.

The more the anointing functions and operates through those who are projecting the mind and will of God, the more those doing so find themselves facing criticism and misunderstandings. These negative reactions usually come from men and women who mean well, but who do not understand God's eternal purposes and His divine plan of progression. These critics are generally still living in a holding pattern of yesterday's former successes with the stubborn belief that, "If it works, don't fix it!"

KEEP PRESSING ON

It is very easy to become satisfied with what you have right now and criticize whatever new thing God is doing for today and for tomorrow. You will notice, however, that those who do this have entered into routine and ritual instead of the dynamics of the unction that God wants to pour forth onto, into and through those who are moving with Him. We all tend to take things for granted. When things are going well, we relax and lean back on our previous victories, telling ourselves that all is well and we have earned a rest. By doing so, the forces of regression begin to creep in. History tells us that throughout the great moves of God over the years, this is what has happened time and again.

Older saints of God can fall into this trap. Sometimes, as we age, we feel that we can rest on our laurels of a life lived for God and sweetly wait out our golden years until we go home. The senior saint that falls into this pattern of thinking is in danger of regression. The closer you get to completing your work for God on earth and the nearer you get to the privilege of going home, the less time there is left for Satan to pull you away from the Lord. His attacks are often stronger, but sneakier, for he knows that he is not dealing with a baby Christian. He plans his attacks carefully, moving in subtle ways.

The senior saint must remain spiritually aware and active, always continuing to press on into God right up until his or her departure date for glory. Your final golden years are a span of time that God has given you to move in closer to Him so that when you step into your new home in heaven, you are going to step confidently into the fullness of what He has promised. He does not want you to step out of this world with any regrets.

Those who have passed the milestone of middle age and have God flowing freely in their spirits can bring a stream of life into any gathering of people they encounter. Spiritual maturity and the wisdom of a life lived fully for God can bring a very special life stream of God into any situation or circumstance that cannot be duplicated by all the machinery of religion in the world.

CHRISTIANS HOLD ALL THE KEYS

We as Christians hold the keys to the destiny of the lives of this generation. The wounded spirits, the drunkenness of the world, the broken homes, the alienated children, the alcoholism, the drugs and the unnatural affections can basically all be laid right on the doorstep of Christianity. Why? Because too many Christians in the church have not gone far enough! The majority of the Church has stopped halfway through its purpose and failed the rest of the world.

You are the only one who can make the choice of stopping halfway or of going on all the way. You can be stopped by somebody's criticism. You can be stopped by another's philosophy. You can be hindered by someone's thinking or doctrine. You can be stopped by a bad experience in a church or with a church leader. Or, you can get into the real life stream of God for yourself and walk straight into the face of the storm, fully able to stand solid and firm under any circumstance, any misunderstanding, any attack or any problem. When you have the unction of the Holy One, you have enough faith and authority in the name of Jesus Christ to break every bondage and obstacle that tries to get in your way.

We as Christians are not here to build an "organization" or a "private club." Christian, get it through your head and your heart that we are here to build lives that can stand up to the challenge of these last days. We are here to meet the tragedies of the hour and the heartaches of the day that are holding our generation in bondage.

Regardless of the seemingly impossible state of the world today, God is still totally in control. Your present state and your future are determined by what you do with God and His Word, not by the circumstances of the world around you.

Too many Christians treat the Gospel as an interesting fiction story—truth as fiction and fiction as truth. The Gospel is the true story of life and death, heaven or hell, happiness or sorrow. It is the only true security left in the world. Money can't buy it, television can't duplicate it and your home and your possessions can't imitate it. You either have God and a life in Him or you don't have any life at all. The person without God may think he or she has life, but what people without God really have is walking death.

When you have the unction of God flowing through a fully submitted and obedient life that is dedicated to serving Him, underlined everything has to bow before that authority in the name of Jesus. When you speak His name as a true child of God, you have the right to claim the unction of the Holy One in your life.

TAKING THE UNCTION TO THE PEOPLE

I was very proud of President Reagan and his true compassion as he spoke in the memorial service for the astronauts who were lost in the explosion of the Challenger early in 1986. Throughout the different tragedies during the years he was in office, he was there with the families who were left behind so he could offer his comfort. As he spoke at the memorial service for the astronauts, he said words similar to these, "We need an occasion like this (speaking of the gathering together at the memorial service) so that we can let our tears flow." There was great wisdom and understanding in these words. We as Christians need to take the unction of God to the hurting people of our generation and create the "occasion" for them to feel the comfort and the love of God and let their tears flow... weeping out their sorrow, weeping out the conviction of the Holy Spirit, weeping out the cleansing of forgiveness.

The unction of the Holy One is understood in our finite minds as the anointing upon someone being used of God, especially when he or she is speaking to other people, witnessing, praying or ministering the spiritual gifts. Truth is powerful, but it does not penetrate darkness by itself. God's Word is truth, but it is when that truth has pierced the spirit of a man or woman being used of God (through the anointing or the unction of the Spirit of God) that they can then express it through their understanding to others and it will be received as a living reality. Only the anointing of the Spirit can make truth a reality in the spirit of a man or woman. The anointing or the unction is what makes the truth of God alive and working within the individual.

In my early years in the ministry, I quickly learned that one of the most important rooms within the church was the prayer room. An hour of prayer by God's people before the Sunday night service would bring a great throb of evangelism, conviction, salvation, liberty, anointing and freshness into the meeting. I have always urged choirs, musical groups and special singers to pray before they ministered. I urged our speakers in the Bible School to spend time in prayer before they spoke or participated in our services. Why? So they would be covered with the anointing or the unction of the Holy Spirit and able to make divine truth alive in the spirits of those who listened to them.

When I go to church, I want my truth on fire. I do not want to receive it on ice. I want it alive and powerful. I want it punctuated with miracles, breakthroughs, joy, worship and praise.

There is no substitute for the unction when you are communicating the Gospel. The unction is entirely the work of the Spirit... it is not enthusiasm... it is not zeal... it is not thunder... it is not excitement. Although those characteristics may be present when the unction of God is flowing, don't mistake them for the unction. Only the understanding of your spirit can recognize the true anointing. The unction can be expressed in quiet words or in loud tones. Its presence can be sensed both in an excited fervour and in total stillness. It brings tears to the eye. It brings changes in ideologies and breaks through the shells of tradition and deadness. It rejuvenates the Christian. It is the unction that is molding the body of Christ into a single unit that is expressive of the living, resurrected Christ.

THE SECRETS OF MINISTRY

In Christian service, the unction is the anointing of the Holy Spirit. Unction separates the ministry or service unto God and qualifies it as His work. It is the one divine enablement by which the ministry can accomplish the peculiar and saving effects of preaching. Without unction, there are no spiritual results accomplished. Without unction, the results and the forces in preaching do not rise above the results of unsanctified speech making. In other words, without an unction, a Gospel service has no more lasting effect than a political rally.

An accomplished preacher or teacher can give you new thoughts, bring positive thinking and intrigue you; but if the unction is not present and operating, then all of the new thoughts and positive thinking in the world will not bring what God wants for you. Too many churches today offer predictable, easy-to-swallow services in beautiful buildings with padded altars and foam-covered pews so that the cross won't feel too heavy.

If he is unable to avoid hearing it at all, then our natural man would prefer to have the Gospel delivered to him in soft, cushiony terms without any hurt to his precious flesh. The unction, however, can slice like a knife. It is like a two-edged sword, cutting on both sides, but healing and restoring as it cuts. It divides asunder soul and spirit, penetrating the deepest thoughts of our inner self. The unction brings conviction to the point that men and women either surrender to God or react passionately against the Word of God and quite often against the one who is bringing it as well.

You will not have any peace in this world until God has everything that He wants from you and that is your total being, your complete surrender of self to Him. He doesn't want what you "have", He wants you. He wants to bless you and in fact, if He could trust you, you would be amazed by what He would do for you. God has to be careful what He gives you, because you might backslide if He gives you too much.

Beneath the surface of what the anointing will produce through our lives, we live with a constant risk of the old nature seeking to raise up things of the carnal life again. Yes, we have reckoned the old man (the old nature) dead... that is our spiritual position. But experientially there is a dying that goes on daily to maintain a constant regression in the old life.

This old life must not be fed; it must be mortified by the power and the work of the Word and the Spirit within us. There is a danger in multiple blessings from God without a corresponding level of spiritual balance and maturity. Without this balance, our old life wants to rise up and take these blessings into the realm of use ordained by the carnal mind instead of by the Spirit.

We must constantly surrender our blessings, spiritual gifts and talents to God. It is imperative to recognize that if we surrender them to our flesh and our old nature takes over, our flesh will begin to manipulate and consume the things of God upon its own lust. Every blessing or gift from God is a new test of our ability to surrender all in order to bring forth a vessel of honour fit for the Master's use.

HOW DOES THE UNCTION COME?

The divine truths of God that come forth under the unction of the Holy Spirit are of great value and importance, individually and collectively. This divine unction is generated through the Word by the Holy Spirit. Spiritual results flow through the Gospel as it is ministered, preached and spread under the unction of God.

There are many things that may appear as unction. Sometimes we think it is zeal or emotion or empathy and compassion. Sometimes we think it is present because there is great excitement or loudness. These things may occur when the unction is working, but they are no guarantee of its presence. These are emotional reactions that can be duplicated by Satan through carnality. The unction is totally unique and cannot be counterfeited by the enemy. Those who are carnal, or in the flesh, can be deceived into thinking the unction of God is working in certain situations because of various characteristics that attempt to counterfeit the moving of God. But when you are walking within the light of the Holy Spirit that you have attained at your level of Christianity, you do not need to be told when the unction of the Holy One is present—you will know.

When only an "appearance" of the unction of God is operating in a service, there will be no penetration into the things of the spirit world, no force to bring about conviction and change hearts and lives. A service without the unction of God may have emotional appeal, enthusiasm and different other manifestations, but there will be no healing balm and no spiritual breakthroughs. Those who came into the service will walk out with the same hurts and sorrows and needs they came in with.

When the unction of the Holy One is at work, everyone either walks out happier or angrier... they walk out with cleansing or with guilt. They walk out with anointing or with bitterness. But there will be a change when the unction has been operating, they will not remain the same as they came in. Either they will surrender to the anointing or they will refuse to come under it and they will reject what God is doing. You can never ignore the unction and the anointing. Something will change, either for the better or for the worse!

The church is a place to bring you into a deeper relationship with God and this cannot be accomplished without His mighty unction. We need to understand that God's unction is not only on the pastor, it is His desire that it also be upon every member of the congregation. When the body of Christ finally begins to go far enough, there will be such unction in the gathering of believers that no one will be able to walk into their presence without entering into a realization of God that is life changing and habit breaking.

The divine unction is a distinguishing feature that separates true Gospel preaching from any other methods of presenting truth. It is what makes truth alive and penetrating, it illuminates and quickens the Word. It quickens the human intellect and enables it to better apprehend the Word.

Remember—without the unction, the Gospel has no more power to propagate itself than any other system of teaching. Unction is the seal of divinity; it puts the power of God into the Gospel. Without unction, the Gospel is left to human intelligence to enforce doctrine and religious principles through natural means and concepts instead of a bringing forth of life through the supernatural power of God.

Without the unction, man tries to build God's kingdom with bondage by bringing men and women into a semblance of truth through legalism. This is what happens when the unction is lost... legalism and bondage are the only ways left to try to control and direct the baser nature of mankind. When legalism and bondage fail, then man tries to use the entertainment system to hold people. When that fails, we see the religious movements begin to move into areas of meditation, mind control and actual forms of occult teachings to hold their people. Every natural source of control and persuasion is used.

Unction is not something that comes from the soul of man. It is not a product of man's will or emotions. It cannot be produced by intellect and knowledge. Unction is something that can only come and flow through the spirit of a man or woman as the Spirit of God dwells deep within them. When a man or woman of God begins to speak under that unction, there is something in their words that is living and able to give life. Just sitting down next to someone with an unction from God can bring an awareness of the presence of God that is indefinable. Conviction comes, healing comes, salvation comes. Every Christian in the body of Christ should be seeking to minister under the unction of God.

THE ANOINTING OIL

In Exodus 30:23-33, we read of the anointing oil which is the symbol of the Holy Spirit for the dedication of the person who is anointed to His service and for His purposes. The Lord gave very specific instructions on how to prepare the anointing oil. He said to take spices—pure myrrh, sweet cinnamon, sweet calamus and cassia—and place them into olive oil, compounding a holy ointment after the art of the apothecary. The perfume of the spices in the oil was symbolic of the sweetness of the Holy Spirit.

Then God said to anoint the tabernacle, the ark, the table, all the vessels, the candlestick, the altar of incense, the altar of burnt offering and the laver, which would sanctify them all so they would be most holy. Then the priests were to take this holy anointing oil and anoint Aaron and his sons, consecrating them that they could minister unto God in the priest's office.

The Holy Spirit has been instructed by the Father for a special work in bringing the body of Christ into its divine purpose. In the studies on the Holy Spirit you will find that the blessed Spirit is under direction of the Father and the Son with a definite mission to prepare men and women for the purposes of the Father. The body of Jesus was prepared for His incarnation when an angel came to Mary and informed her that she would form that body within her own, but that the life within that little babe would be the life of the Father.

The Holy Spirit knows the intent and the mind of Christ in order to bring forth what He wants to do within the life of each individual to bring them into the likeness and image of Himself. The Holy Spirit is prepared to administer the life of Jesus in us to bring us into the presence of God. The unction of God is the pouring out of the holy anointing oil by the Holy Spirit.

THE RESULTS OF THIS UNCTION

Many of our problems exist because we haven't taken authority over the enemy who is constantly working to invade our lives, our homes and our families. You can go to church every day, be counselled over and over, be taught by the greatest teachers and be very spiritual; but until you begin to exercise the unction in your life, you will never enter into an overcoming Christian life with full victory.

Don't settle for just getting into heaven to be one of the many believers who will be waving palm branches as the bride of Christ goes into the marriage supper of the Lamb. There will be the overcomers who will be in the bride of Christ and there will be the attendants to the wedding party, the palm branch wavers. Your character as an overcomer must be established here on earth, because you won't get any more character building opportunities when you get to heaven. It takes persistence and resistance here on earth to establish your character. The persistence is supplied by you and the resistance is supplied by the devil. It is the devil who provides the circumstances and situations that build our character as we rise above them and overcome them.

We have been given a span of time in which the mysteries of the Gospel that have been hid from generations and ages shall now be made manifest. Paul was caught up into the heavens and there the Spirit revealed to him all that was in the heart of the Father and the Son that would bring the Church into being. He wrote it into the pages of the Bible by the quickening of the Holy Spirit and then its truth was hidden from the natural mind.

The early Church in the New Testament moved into a great and glorious spiritual body, but then deterioration came as spoken of in the Book of Revelation. Later in history the Holy Spirit began to breathe afresh into the Church and a new hope and spiritual strength was restored, salvation was restored and a powerful movement formed. Then the Holy Spirit revealed that there was a restoration of divine healing and the other spiritual gifts and another movement came into being. He revealed that there was more in sanctification and another movement was formed.

We had Lutherans, Presbyterians, Wesleyans and Methodists. Then one day, the Holy Spirit jumped right into the middle of all of them. There began to be a new breathing of the Spirit within the different churches around the turning of this century. Sad to say, they did not understand it and the result was schism and division that has not been really bridged yet.

God did a mighty gleaning on the Church over half a century ago and out of that gleaning came the Pentecostal movement from all walks of life. I heard an interesting, but sad phrase recently—Pentecostal humanism. The powerful, life-giving Pentecostal movement is battling some of its own schisms today and God is now gleaning the Pentecostal movement.

He is gleaning the true believer from every religious bondage and bringing them unto Himself in these last days. The Song of Solomon says, "Who is this that cometh up from the wilderness, leaning on her beloved?" (Song of Solomon 8:5) This is as the Church will be, coming up out of the wilderness of the world, leaning upon the arm of her beloved Christ. God is beginning to lead us out, taking us by the hand, taking us by our circumstances, taking us for His own.

He is beginning to melt our wilfulness, bending us and molding us. He is letting every well around us go dry until the only water supply we can find to quench our cry for fulfillment is the living water He offers. God is beginning to do His final work in this generation and He is going to complete that which He has begun in us. There is nothing hell can do that can take away from what God has planned. It can only cause us to be crowded closer to draw more of His precious supply of living water.

Radiance will begin to shine through these believers as this is the period known of in Ephesians 4:8-15 when the Holy Spirit shall bring about the maturity of the body of Christ through the five-fold ministry gifts for the maturing of Jesus' body into His likeness and image. The body is coming into unity and being made one through the mystery of the Gospel being revealed in the unveiling of Jesus. God is bringing unity, for He is not ruled by denominations. His only interest is whether we are in Christ or in Adam and in whether we have His life within our spirits or not.

We are writing our own ticket today, our church isn't going to write it for us. Our ticket to heaven is going to come out of the Word, it is going to come out of prayer and it is going to come out of commitment to God. If we don't write the right ticket, we will pay for our travels with tears, broken homes, unsaved loved ones left behind, sickness and poverty.

God is gleaning His people out of the crowds who say they are Christians, but who never knew Him. It has become fashionable to say that you are a born-again Christian, but it has not become fashionable to live the committed, dedicated life of one. Then there are many Christians who will fight for what Jesus said two thousand years ago, but they cannot hear what He is saying today.

America has heard so much religion that it is becoming immune to the Gospel and the mighty movements of yesterday have become dignified and sophisticated. Men and women today are still trying to get power without holiness, without conviction and weeping and without surrender. They are trying to do it man's way. Who cares about dignity and sophistication when all around us people are dying? What we need to care about are results! The unction of God brings results.

God wants to separate you and I for a distinct purpose. He wants to use us in powerful ways with the anointing and the unction flowing through each one of us. Don't worry about whether you're worthy or strong enough; just cast yourself at the feet of Jesus and He will take care of the rest. Your past is under the blood and you're forgiven, clean and washed. Your failures are finished and your future can be completely victorious in Christ. Remember that God doesn't deal with you according to your past, your sins or your failures; He deals with you according to the incorruptible seed of Christ's life that is now residing in you.

THE CONVICTING POWER OF THE UNCTION

When the anointing and the unction is really flowing, sin becomes <u>SIN</u>. It so hurts in your spirit that it can be compared to the feeling of a piece of sand in your eye... if it isn't removed, it just gets worse and worse and the tears flow. You know that you can't run away from the speck of sand in your eye, it will only run right with you. You must deal with it and have it removed.

Now consider this: when you have had a painful piece of dirt in your eye and cried out to someone to help you remove it, did they condemn you and judge you for the stupidity and foolishness of getting dirt in your eye in the first place? Or, did they try to help you remove it as quickly as possible?

Don't run away from Jesus when He convicts you of sin by the unction of the Holy Spirit... run towards Him. He stands with open arms to forgive and to cleanse and to remove the offending sin. Jesus does not stand waiting for you with judgment; He stands waiting with compassion, tenderness, forgiveness, help and healing.

CHAPTER 6

BREAKING THE YOKE WITH THE ANOINTING

We live in a world that is filled with philosophies, ideologies, religious concepts and various other ideas of men taken from partial teachings of the Word. These "partial-truth based" philosophies and ideas have resulted in a bondage of fear that prevents many from moving into the full realities of truth that God has for us.

This same fear and caution has prevented many from entering into a relationship with God that the anointing of the Holy Spirit might be manifested in and through their lives. They have held back because of personal failures and doubts or criticisms and judgmental opinions of others until they find themselves cornered, unsure and convinced that they are unworthy of being a vehicle of God's blessing unto others.

There are so many Christians who walk around with a heart that is open, a determined smile on their face and an intense desire to serve and love God; yet inside they are longing and aching for God to do the things that they have reached for in prayer for so long. They don't realize that Jesus has already broken the yoke of bondage that would keep them from receiving the answers to their prayers for unsaved loved ones, healing, financial deliverance and other needs. We don't need to break the yoke of bondage, He has already broken it. The problem lies in our receiving the freedom and the deliverance from the yoke and in our appropriating the provisions that God has made for us.

There is a yearning in the heart of the world today as well as the cry in the heart of the Christian. Each Christian of this hour knows that there is far more for God's children than we have laid hold of, there is far more that He has already provided for us as His people. There are those who have appropriated some of these provisions, but many have not laid hold of any of them.

The ultimate end of the Gospel is the restoration of what has been lost. God wants us prepared and able to receive His glory and His presence, to be restored into perfect fellowship with Him. That is what we really all want, too, because one minute of His presence is worth a lifetime of living.

The unction is God's divine enablement, by the anointing of the Holy Spirit, to accomplish this purpose of the Gospel in the lives of men and women. The Church is to be a vehicle, the body through which a flow of this life and anointing can be manifested. Jesus intended that it would flow through His entire body. The unction or the anointing is the very thing that is the secret of deliverance, changes, the breaking down of barriers, the breaking of the yokes and the eliminating of sin in lives.

The virtue of the Son of God is as great today as when He raised the dead and healed the sick during His years of ministry as He walked on this earth in human form. He hasn't changed; the virtue and the power have only become mightier since He died on the cross, rose again, took back the keys of the kingdom and stepped forth to say, "I am the resurrection and the life." The problem is not with Jesus or with the Gospel, the problem is in the believer. Too many believers are careless with, even to the point of deliberately ignoring, the spiritual things that could bring forth tremendous life and healing and restoration in their lives and the lives of others.

THE POWER OF THE ANOINTING

The anointing is always associated in the Word with the Spirit and the power of the Word being so forceful as spoken of in Hebrews 4:12, "For the word of God is quick, and powerful, and sharper than any twoedged sword piercing even to the dividing asunder of soul and spirit, and of the joints and marrow, and a discerner of the thoughts and intents of the heart." When the Word is quickened and made powerful, it is because of an anointing or unction.

The anointing is a divine quickening that is released from the Holy Spirit through the one speaking as the Word is communicated to bring life and reality to an individual or to an audience. This anointing, when it is manifested through the one who is ministering, will be felt by the individual who is listening. The anointing can be "felt" spiritually, emotionally, mentally or even physically, through one or all of these channels.

The writer of the epistle to the Ephesians shows us two things in chapter 1:17-18, "That the God of our Lord Jesus Christ, the Father of glory, may give unto you the spirit of wisdom and revelation in the knowledge of him. The eyes of your understanding being enlightened; that ye may know what is the hope of his calling, and what the riches of the glory of his inheritance in the saints."

He is speaking to the Church in Ephesus in verse 17 when he says, "that the Father of glory may give unto you the spirit of wisdom and (the spirit of) revelation in the knowledge of him." Why? For the purpose in verse 18 that, "The eyes of your understanding being enlightened; that ye may know what is the hope of his calling and what the riches of the glory of his inheritance in the saints."

We can listen without hearing and we can look without seeing. Truth can be truth on fire or truth on ice. The difference lies in the unction of the Spirit working through the one who speaks and the anointing of the Spirit of God upon the listener.

The Spirit can cause the receptive faculties of the spirits and souls of men and women to receive the truth's power that will awaken them, produce conviction of sin, reveal that their deep hungering is for God and bring about a willingness to submit self to God. The power of the anointing of the Spirit can bring about all of these breakthroughs and more in the hardest of hearts even when it is completely contrary to the will of the natural man.

THE MIGHTY YOKE BREAKER

Isaiah 10:27 says, "And it shall come to pass in that day, that his burden shall be taken away from off thy shoulder, and his yoke from off thy neck and the yoke shall be destroyed because of the anointing." Isaiah was speaking to Israel of what the Lord was going to do. Israel was under the heel of the Assyrians because of their disobedience, neglect, wilfulness and refusal to step out to be who God wanted them to be.

They became careless, taking for granted God's promises that He had chosen them to be the people who would manifest Him to the world. So God allowed them to come under the heel of the Assyrians, a nation He called the rod of His anger (Isaiah 10:5 NIV). The Assyrians looted and plundered and brought destruction upon the Israelites, placing a burden upon them that was unbearable.

In the Hebrew language, the word yoke can either be used figuratively or literally as an absolute reality. But when we are under a yoke, it is a yoke either way, a bondage and a pressure brought to bear that can press down on our lives until we are heavy hearted, burdened, stripped and crushed by circumstances. The yoke will exact a price from us that minimizes or limits our motivation until we feel more like weeping than smiling, our steps become heavy and we feel like we cannot go on. Have you ever found yourself saying, "I can't go on like this anymore, I have prayed for so long, I have been faithful, I have tithed, I have read the Word, I have regularly attended church and I have always honoured you, God. Why haven't you answered me and delivered me from this bondage? Often we feel the need to tell God something we think He doesn't already know and perhaps that will make the difference.

Giving God "unknown information" doesn't make the difference... our laying hold of our provisions and the freedom already provided for us at the time that Jesus broke the yoke is what makes the difference.

Isaiah 10:27 says that God did not take the yoke away, He destroyed the yoke because of the anointing. The enemy cannot replace what God has destroyed. As we allow Scripture to speak forth into today from that period of time in the history of Israel, we see that the enemy's power is broken. Deliverance was in the making at that point. Yet man, even in the religious realm, has lost this understanding and has regressed in his inward spiritual motivation, thereby reverting to all kinds of bondage.

We know of the great revivals that have come and gone in the church world. We have all read about the tremendous things that have happened and the marvellous outpourings of the Spirit of God that brought different spiritual movements into being. Then, in order to "maintain" that flow and the reality of what the moving of the Spirit of God has brought into being, what happens? Man, usually with good intent and purpose, tries to bring in regulations, by-laws and rituals to maintain what God has already done! How often we forget there is another way—His way!

Through man's ways, kingdoms begin to be built, pure motivation is lost and fences rise. Bondages are placed on the people to keep them inside the fences until some Christians become like little tin soldiers, marching doggedly ahead, stiff-legged and straight-armed, fearful of wandering outside of the protection of their doctrinal walls.

We need to return to the understanding that when the Son sets you free, you are free indeed. Knowing the truth of this is what sets you free. God wants you to live by His light, not by your own light. He has an anointing and a flow of life and power for His people so that all Christians can live in freedom and without fear or bondage.

I used to shock my Bible School students by telling them that I was so free that I did all the bad things I wanted to and I went to all the wrong places that I wanted to... but the key was, I didn't want to. The "want to" just wasn't there.

As a child of God, we have a new nature that is choosy about what it feeds on. This new nature doesn't want food out of the garbage cans or the dumping grounds of this world. We are living in this world, but our appetites don't have to be of this world. This new nature needs strong, pure, powerful, spiritual food to nourish it. Too many churches have lowered their standards of spiritual feeding to satisfy the level of the carnal hunger of the people. Instead, they should be lifting the level of their hunger so that the people could learn to feed upon the things of God. This is the only kind of feeding that will build a strong, godly life on the inside of men and women. Instead, these churches have reinforced the acceptance of a lukewarm life that so many have become accustomed to believing as being all there is to Christianity.

BREAKING THE YOKE OF BONDAGE

In the ninth chapter of Isaiah, the prophet makes the great annunciation of the birth of Jesus, "For unto us a child is born, unto us a son is given; and the government shall be upon his shoulder; and his name shall be called Wonderful, Counsellor, The mighty God, The everlasting Father, The Prince of Peace. Of the increase of his government and peace there shall be no end, upon the throne of David, and upon his kingdom, to order it, and to establish it with judgment and with justice from henceforth even for ever. The zeal of the Lord of hosts will perform this" (Isaiah 9:6-7).

Chapter 11 continues to describe the Messiah, Jesus, beginning with, "And there shall come forth a rod out of the stem of Jesse, and a Branch shall grow out of his roots; and the spirit of the Lord shall rest upon him, the spirit of wisdom and understanding, the spirit of counsel and might, the spirit of knowledge and of the fear of the Lord; and shall make him of quick understanding in the fear of the Lord; and he shall not judge after the sight of his eyes, neither reprove after the hearing of his ears; but with righteousness shall he judge the poor, and reprove with equity for the meek of the earth; and he shall smite the earth with the rod of his mouth, and with the breath of his lips shall he slay the wicked. And righteousness shall be the girdle of his loins, and faithfulness the girdle of his reins" (Isaiah 11:1-5).

Chapter fourteen of Isaiah begins to speak of the anointing breaking the yoke of the enemy upon God's people. "The anointing shall break the yoke" is speaking of deliverance from the Assyrians who had taken over the nation of Israel at that time, placing them under bondage to pay large sums of money in taxes, demanding things from them that brought them into a heavily burdened life. Notice that God says in Isaiah 14:25-26, "I will break the Assyrians in my land, and upon my mountains tread him under foot; then shall his yoke depart from off them, and his burden depart from off their shoulders. This is the purpose that is purposed upon the whole earth; and this is the hand that is stretched out upon all the nations." What exactly is being said here? How will the yoke of the enemy be broken?

In referring to the word "yoke," let us look at Matthew 11:29-30, "Take my yoke upon you, and learn of me; for I am meek and lowly in heart; and ye shall find rest unto your souls. For my yoke is easy and my burden is light." This is the yoke that is placed upon mankind by Christ.

The yoke of the enemy is harsh and heavy and the Assyrians had placed Israel under great bondage by forcing them into a severe condition of servitude with no hope of getting out. "The anointing shall break the yoke" refers not only to the bondage that was upon Israel, but also to the yoke of the enemy that is upon the whole world.

Syria, land of the Assyrians, represents the world with its godless intentions, its war and its desire to bring mankind into servitude.

This is the spirit of the world today which has brought over fifty percent of the nations in the world into war and servitude.

Sin brings man into servitude, into a bondage in which he serves sin until he finds himself in circumstances that are beyond his ability to break. He can be in bondage to alcohol, to lust, to a government, to attitudes and to many other things. The spirit of the Assyrians is the same spirit that is bringing men and women into bondage and servitude today, it is only being carried out in different dimensions.

God said He was going to break the Assyrians and that He would deal with them and crush them upon the mountain, treading them under His foot. He said that the yoke would depart off from Israel... that same yoke that Jesus has come to take off His people and from this generation. Isaiah 10:27 brings to our attention that the yoke of bondage would be broken by the anointing which refers to Christ; it was He who would come to break the bondage upon mankind in order to give men and women a whole new way of life. That anointing is here and it is breaking the yoke upon the multitudes of people who have received Christ. Upon the reception of Jesus into the heart of a man or woman, the Spirit of God does His work within that individual's heart to bring to pass God's promises from centuries ago.

For an illustration of how God destroyed the Assyrians (the enemy), let us look at chapters 36 and 37 of Isaiah where Sennacherib comes to attack Jerusalem and King Hezekiah. King Hezekiah had been wayward and in sin, but at this point in time he had made his repentance before God. Hezekiah had rebuilt the altars that he had torn down and reestablished his relationship in obedience to God. The prophet Isaiah gave him encouragement and said, "He shall not come into this city, not shoot an arrow there, nor come before it with shields, nor cast a bank against it. By the way that he came, by the same shall he return and shall not come into this city, saith the Lord. For I will defend this city to save it for mine own sake, and for my servant David's sake. Then the agent of the Lord went forth, and smote the camp of the Assyrians a hundred and fourscore and five thousand; and when they arose early in the morning, behold, they were all dead corpses. So Sennacherib king of Assyria departed, and went and returned, and dwelt at Nineveh. And it came to pass, as he was worshipping in the house of Nisroch his god, that Adrammelech and Sharezer his sons smote him with the sword; and they escaped in the land of Armenia; and Esarhaddon his son reigned in his stead" (Isaiah 37:33-38).

2 Chronicles 32:21 tells the same story of the Lord saving Hezekiah and the inhabitants of Jerusalem from the hand of King Sennacherib and the Assyrians. He sent an angel which cut off the mighty soldiers and leaders of the camp of the Assyrians. He sent the King of Assyria back, full of shame, to his own land. When Sennacherib came into the house of his god, his sons which had come forth of his own loins slew him with a sword.

God fulfilled His promise to the Israelites by killing 185,000 Assyrian soldiers in their sleep (Isaiah 37:36). He broke the Assyrian's yoke just as He had said, "The anointing shall break the yoke." This is exactly what He will do for all those who trust Him. Do you have bondages in your life that are more powerful than 185,000 Assyrian warriors waiting to destroy you? Whatever the bondage may be, that anointing of Jesus Christ is sufficient.

Jesus is the Anointer who was to come and who has come. This promise in the Old Testament is fulfilled for you and me in the new covenant in Christ which belongs to us as Christians.

THE GOD OF THE OLD TESTAMENT IS THE SAME GOD OF THE NEW TESTAMENT

God manifested His presence in the Old Testament by many means and supernatural acts. By a supernatural act of God, the River Jordan divided... the Red Sea parted... a rock in the desert suddenly spilled forth water... flocks of quail descended upon the Israelites for food when they were unhappy with the manna. Daniel was safe and sound in the lion's den and the Hebrew children walked unharmed in the fiery furnace.

The scene changed in the New Testament and a new life flowed that did not come by the law, for the law could not give life. Jesus, the Anointed One, came. He often manifested supernatural acts, but that was not His primary purpose for being on earth. The Spirit of God brought forth His Son to change the very nature of man and put a life within him that he never had before.

2 Peter 1:4 says, "Whereby are given unto us exceeding great and precious promises; that by these ye might be partakers of the divine nature, having escaped the corruption that is in the world through lust." Every man and woman has been born into this world with a fallen and perverted nature, born without any divine life. This is hard for many to grasp as they gaze into the sweet, innocent face of a newborn baby... how could that tiny, precious life have a fallen nature?

The only way that sweet, newborn baby will ever escape the ravages of sin is to receive the entrance of the life of Christ within his or her spirit, the regeneration that only occurs with the implantation of the incorruptible seed. This is why it is so important to guide and teach little children in the ways of the Lord from the very beginning, covering them with prayer and protection through the name of Jesus until they are old enough to choose to accept that gift of life from Christ themselves. We as parents, family and caring Christians affect that choice with our prayers and intercession and shaping of their young lives through example and teaching... but ultimately it is a choice that they must make with their own will.

In this day and age there is preaching and teaching of the Gospel like never before and the Holy Spirit is working and gathering in people by many acts of power. Churches have been built, Christian schools have been established and there have been all different manners and ways of meeting the crises in human lives. But there is an ever-increasing rise of resistance to the Gospel around the world as the enemy is stepping up his attacks as the final spiritual conflict in time is drawing to a close.

Satan is covering all the bases and if he can't get us from the outside, he will try to get us from the inside. He will try to get us to nullify the Word of God and its power and bring an end to the freedom of what this Gospel can do within the heart of a person.

SATAN'S ALL OUT FINAL ATTACK

As we move on to the end of this age, there are all kinds of bondages and pressures that are being placed upon men and women who have entered into the reality of a living, resurrected Christ. This is the final attack of the enemy to try to defeat the Gospel through Christians who are in the body of Christ. He cannot defeat Christ, but he can try to defeat those who believe in Him.

We must understand that if we are a child of God, a new life is within us. You have been born again and the Anointed One dwells inside of you. Jesus said, "Come unto me, all ye that labour and are heavy laden, and I will give you rest. Take my yoke upon you, and learn of me; for I am meek and lowly in heart; and ye shall find rest unto your souls. For my yoke is easy, and my burden is light" (Matthew 11:28-30). Jesus is telling us that while there is a yoke of bondage, there is also the yoke of relationship with Him. He wants us not to be yoked with the world, but to be yoked with Him. In other words, He will carry our burden. His yoke is easier than the world's yoke which is full of heaviness, darkness and pressure.

The enemy has been on your trail ever since you committed your life to Christ, but the burden he wants to put upon you does not belong to you. Jesus has broken that yoke and He wants you to realize that you are tied together with Him in a yoke that He will bear with you, making it easy for you. Jesus is promising "in writing" in Matthew 11:28-30 that He will take you through whatever you face if you will only yoke yourself together with Him.

Today we are living on the threshold of the edge of time. Jesus is soon to return and even though the world may not understand this, the world knows it is true. The devil realizes the truth of this more than some Christians seem to. Satan knows that final and permanent things are happening right now that are extremely detrimental to his plans. This is why he has increased the intensity of his attack to capture all of the souls that he can to banish them to darkness forever. He knows the truth of the divine plan and purpose.

REMEMBER—THE YOKE IS BROKEN

In the last days we know that many things will happen, just like we are now seeing all over the world—terrible floods, famines, earthquakes, volcanic eruptions, wars, devastating accidents causing the loss of hundreds of lives, uprisings and rampant evil. What is this doing to people in the day in which we live?

One of the strongest yokes of bondage that people are living under today is fear. It is so easy to come under this bondage in our tormented society. Fear is a real torture, but perfect love casts out fear. "There is no fear in love; but perfect love casteth out fear; because fear hath torment..." (1 John 4:18). Also, "...God has not given us the spirit of fear; but of power, and of love, and of a sound mind... Who (God) hath saved us, and called us with an holy calling, not according to our works, but according to his own purpose and grace, which was given us in Christ Jesus before the world began" (2 Timothy 1:7, 9).

Fear is linked to the bondages of pressure, stress and anxiety. Today there is pressure involved in the act of merely surviving in the world; there is great pressure on jobs and heartbreaking pressure within families torn asunder by alcohol, drugs and Satanic influences. There is the anxiety over children who are going astray, lured by the bright lights of the world and captivated by temporary escape in drugs and entertainment as they seek to relieve their own pressures and anxieties.

There is the yoke of poverty and financial stress. Poverty, whether financial, spiritual, emotional or physical, is all the devil's business. God does not want you trapped under the bondage of poverty; He wants to meet your need. If you are fighting poverty, there may be spiritual warfare involved. Sometimes there has been disobedience and sometimes there is lack of good judgment involved. There is a need for discernment when dealing with the yoke of poverty, because you need to know whether you are battling spiritual warfare that is not of your own making or whether you have allowed the bondage to enter though your own disobedience to God's principles of finance and obedience as put forth in the Word. The spiritual warfare will still be necessary, but you need to have a special spiritual awareness so that you can learn what God would teach you through the circumstances to avoid future pitfalls in this area.

There are yokes of unhappy marriages, broken homes, religious ideologies, sickness and disease, disobedience to God's Word, misunderstanding, wounded spirits, depression, loneliness, guilt, condemnation and prejudice. These are only some of the bondages that Satan brings upon people through the circumstances of their lives. God wants you to live in victory over your circumstances, rising above them and becoming so strong in Christ that Satan does not stand a chance to use them against you. God has predestined you to achieve victory over the circumstances that the curse has brought upon this world. The curse came through Adam, but the victory came through Christ.

IS THE CURSE HOLDING YOU DOWN?
OR
IS THE VICTORY LIFTING YOU UP?

Are you living with the spirit of Adam within you or are you living with the Spirit of Christ within you?

You can rejoice in the midst of all your troubles for the yokes that Satan would put upon you are already broken. The whole answer to why you can't seem to get out of the bondage is that you have not received what is provided. I know most of you have sincerely tried, but you have not gone far enough.

"Now he which stablisheth us with you in Christ, and hath anointed us, is God" (1 Corinthians 1:21). God has anointed us, we have the Anointed One within us. The anointing is what accomplishes the following.

"The Spirit of the Lord God is upon me, because the Lord hath anointed me to preach good tidings unto the meek; he hath sent me to bind up the brokenhearted, to proclaim liberty to the captives and the opening of the prison to them that are bound; to proclaim the acceptable year of the Lord, and the day of vengeance of our God; to comfort all that mourn; to appoint unto them that mourn in Zion, to give unto them beauty for ashes, the oil of joy for mourning, the garment of praise for the spirit of heaviness; that they might be called the trees of righteousness, the planting of the Lord, that he might be glorified. And they shall build the old wastes, they shall raise up the former desolations, and they shall repair the waste cities, the desolations of many generations" (Isaiah 61:1-4).

God has a divine purpose to press into our spirits the very fruits of the Anointed One for He has anointed us to carry out the very things that He was raised up for. We are to be the vehicles of His divine purpose. Isaiah 61:6 says, "Ye shall be named the Priests of the Lord; men shall call you the ministers of our God; ye shall eat the riches of the Gentiles, and in their glory shall ye boast yourselves."

God has promised us this and He does not break His promises. Don't look at the bigness of your need; look at the bigness of your God, for He is the yoke breaker. We don't have to break the yoke, it is already done. When Jesus came out of His tomb on resurrection morning and ascended unto our Father to present His sacrifice which the Father accepted, every yoke that the world and its system can ever put upon man through the enemy of our soul was broken and nullified. The yoke is broken and now God wants us to possess our possessions.

Whether you feel free or not, you are free! Don't look at the results or seeming lack of results, look at the yoke breaker. Look at what the Word says He has provided and claim it. Claim it again and again and again. It belongs to you.

Determine in your spirit that you will not allow yourself to live under the heel of the oppressor—that is your <u>choice</u> to make... not Satan's! There may be quite a battle with him; there might be heavy spiritual warfare to convince him you have finally decided to claim what has been yours all along. But between the prayer and the answer, God will make a saint out of you as you rise above the hindrances that have had you fenced in for so long. You will speak differently and your tongue will no longer rattle off unbelief. Neither will your spirit bring condemnation upon someone else. You will no longer pack a briefcase around with you that is full of prejudice and negativity.

You will see victory in every tear; you will see victory even in the grave. You will see the victory in seeming defeat; you will see the victory in sickness and in healing. You will see victory in that which seems negative because when He finally gets this truth through to you, you are going to have a yoke-breaking marathon. You will enter into a greater dimension of God until you know that you know that you know that the God you serve really is who He says He is!

ROOT CAUSES OF MANY DISEASES

Many of the yokes that God's people have not shaken off are the root cause of the diseases and sicknesses they have. If you live with a troubled spirit and a burdened heart, under the heel of depression, sickness takes root in your spirit and then moves outward to affect your body. When this happens, many other consequences result as well as physical illness. One of the most interesting books I have read regarding sickness and disease, NONE OF THESE DISEASES, was written by a doctor. In this book, he clearly defines many illnesses and sicknesses that are associated with spiritual bondages within our own life. He was well aware of the truth that the greater the spiritual life flow is in our spirit, the greater our ability is to overcome the bondages and the yokes that the devil is trying to attach to us.

We must never forget that the anointing not only breaks the yokes, but it destroys them and the enemy hasn't the power to put them back on us unless we help him. We keep ourselves free from cooperation with the enemy and his works by a good relationship with God. When our relationship is right and clean and open before God, we can stand firm and say, "I will not be defeated by any of the pressures of these last days that are trying to bring me into the bondages of the endtime period. I have the Anointed One within me and I am anointed to break any yoke that dares to raise its head in my presence! Praise the name of the Lord."

If someone wants to live in defeat, they will get all the help they want. If they want to be disobedient and live in regret, Satan will provide plenty of slick spots in the road to help them slide into a fall and every soft chair of self-pity and discouragement they could possibly want to burrow down into. If someone wants to neglect God's word and put it aside on the shelf; that is their privilege. But there isn't a single one of God's children who cannot move in and lay hold of the truth of victorious living in the anointing of God if they want to! Those who press in harder and see the truth sooner should extend a hand with the proof of the truth of the anointing and its power to break yokes back to their brothers and sisters who are still living in defeat.

When Jesus stood in the synagogue in Nazareth and read from the book of Isaiah, "The Spirit of the Lord is upon me, because he hath anointed me to preach the gospel to the poor; he hath sent me to heal the brokenhearted, to preach deliverance to the captives and recovering of sight to the blind, to set at liberty them that are bruised, to preach the acceptable year of the Lord" (Luke 4:18-19), He was giving an affirmation to Isaiah 61.

He knew everything that was going to be happening in these days, He knew the price that you and I would have to pay in these times. He knew all of the things that this age would bring upon us.

Herein lies the secret of the administrative work of the Spirit of God. Jesus said in John 7:38, "He that believeth on me, as the scripture hath said, out of his belly shall flow rivers of living water." You have a life inside of you, His life, and there is to be living water flowing out from you. When you see someone who is weak, it is you who should be the strong one. When you see someone who is depressed or discouraged, it is you who should be the one full of hope and encouragement. You have the anointing to bring hope and to reveal that the yoke is already broken so they do not have to live under its defeat.

We may not fully understand how the Holy Spirit works through us to administer that life of Christ, but we don't need to know "how." We only need to accept the truth that He does! We have the One who anoints, the Spirit of God, God the Son, God the Father, God the Holy Spirit, inside of us! We're a whole troop of mighty spiritual warriors all by ourselves when we have the Trinity in us. We never go into battle alone!

We have the authority of Christ through the anointing of God when we dare to move into the promises of God. When we decide to fully trust in that authority and anointing and step out on His Word, God can animate us with such divine light that the rest of the world will wonder what is the matter with us. We can bring authority, hope, light, truth and deliverance through the anointing and the power of the Gospel.

When Jesus spoke to the Samaritan woman with the shattered romances who was guilty of adultery and many sins, confessions were made and the guilt was gone. When Jesus spoke to the man with the spirit of infirmity by the pool of Bethesda who had been laying waiting for a healing for thirty-eight years, the man arose with a whole, healthy body. When Jesus spoke to the lepers who were dying of that terrible disease, they were healed. When the woman with the issue of blood touched the hem of His garment, the issue dried up.

Jesus spoke and said," I am the bread of life, I am the water of life, I am the truth, I am the resurrection… I am the Alpha and the Omega, the beginning and the end. I am the hope of your tomorrow; I am your sustenance today. I am what I have said and I have broken the yoke. Will you not receive that truth and live in the freedom of what I have provided for you?"

The name of Jesus is above every other name… it knows no limits and it is your family name. You are His family and you have every right to use the family name to bring the anointing to others, in fact it is your responsibility to do so.

The whole world is reaching for something and someone who can give them hope. They are reaching for men and women who have moved far enough into God to show them how to receive their freedom and their liberty from Christ.

Many have become the sad product of man's religious, doctrinal ideas instead of the truths of the Word. Don't fall into that trap; don't give your ideas to the people reaching out to you for help—give them the Word of God. Use the anointing that is upon you when you have the Anointed One flowing freely forth from inside to help them receive the truth of the Gospel.

Christian, claim your possessions! Stake out your promises, they belong to you. If you had been living in the gold rush days of California's history and found a place where there was gold, you would have staked your claim and declared that it now belonged to you. If someone tried to take it from you, you would have grabbed a gun and chased them off. The promises of God throughout the Word are pure gold just waiting for you to find them, nuggets of gold freely available to everyone who seeks them in faith and stakes their claim on them. When Satan comes to kill and to steal and to try to jump your claim on your gold in the Word of God, grab your spiritual guns and run him clear over the next hill.

Remember this, "We have not received the spirit of the world, but the Spirit who is from God, that we may understand what God has freely given us" (1 Corinthians 2:12). If you aren't receiving a clear message from the Spirit of God as to where your claims are to His gold in the Word, perhaps the spirit of the world is coming in too loud. You may need to adjust your spiritual antenna and fine tune your receiver with prayer and the Word. Those two spiritual "technicians" are guaranteed to give new life and power to old batteries and weak receivers.

CHAPTER 7

ADORNING THE BRIDE

God knew that the law could not make people live in righteousness. Galatians 3:19 tells us that "…it (the law) was added because of transgressions, till the seed should come to whom the promise was made…" The law only had the power to show man what was wrong with him; it could not give him the power needed to live a holy life. This power was revealed through Jesus Christ. It is a power that is freely available to any man, woman, young person or child who chooses to accept Him as their Saviour and receive the implantation of His life within their spirit. It is through this power revealed in us by Jesus indwelling our spirit that we, as Christians, can attain the holiness and the blemish-free life necessary to become a part of the bride of Christ.

Out of God's eternal plan came His decree that His Son would have a bride without spot or wrinkle, holy and without blemish. Ephesians 5:25 says, "Husbands, love your wives, even as Christ also loved the church, and gave himself for it; that he might sanctify and cleanse it with the washing of water by the word, that he might present it to himself a glorious church, not having spot, or wrinkle, or any such thing; but it should be holy and without blemish."

The Holy Spirit came into the world to dwell in bodies made clean by the cleansing blood of Jesus Christ. Then He began His work to prepare these people, the Christians, to become part of the bride for Jesus. We do not know now why God chose to do it this way, for this is the mystery of Godliness. All we know is that this is God's plan and this is the work that the Holy Spirit is doing now, He is bringing the body of Christ into holiness and readiness for marriage to the Lamb of God.

God chose Israel in His divine planning as the nation with many covenant blessings that was to come forth out of Abraham. It was Israel that was to show the one true God to the world. There were many false gods in that day. And so, God had to raise up Israel to reveal Himself to the world as the one and only true God.

There was an unusual relationship between Israel and God which is illustrated in the book of Hosea. The prophet Hosea speaks of the unfaithful wife, an illustration of Israel who was married to God. The reference to this relationship shows Israel as God's wife, not as His bride. However, Israel turned in apostasy from God which is spiritual adultery. No longer was Israel revealing the one true God to the world as He had chosen them to do. The covenants that He has made with Israel will be fulfilled exactly as He has said they would, but He has had to deal with Israel first in order to bring them back into a right relationship with Him.

In the New Testament God is manifested in a different way through Christ. God was not limited to working only through Israel; rather He now prepared a new and living way to express Himself to the world through Christ and through the preaching of the Gospel which is both the living and the written Word. This Gospel is preached by the power and the anointing of the Holy Spirit to gather a people unto God from out of the world… a peculiar people, a holy nation, composed not only of the Gentiles, but the Israelites as well.

Remember, there are three forces in the human race in this world. One force is the unconverted Jews, the second force is the unconverted Gentiles and the third force is the holy nation (the body of Christ) which is the result of the preaching of the Gospel—the Jews and the Gentiles who have become converted and brought into the body of Christ. Satan works through the first two forces, the unconverted Jews and Gentiles, trying to bring pressure and defeat upon the third force. The Holy Spirit works through the last force, God's holy nation, the chosen generation as spoken of in 1 Peter 2:9, to bring truth and life to the first two forces. Thus the Church, the body of Christ, the believers with the new nature become the avenue of expression to the world of God the Father, God the Son and God the Holy Spirit.

THE CALL OF THE SPIRIT

You cannot "join" this group of people who will be the bride, you cannot "earn" a position in the bride, nor can you "buy" your way into the bride. You do not choose to become a part; you must be born into the bride of Christ by a spiritual birth. Neither can you choose the time when you will finally submit and answer His call to become a part of the bride—you must answer when the Holy Spirit draws you. He will not always call and He will not always speak… be full of gratitude when the Holy Spirit is drawing and dealing with you. Men and women cannot refuse the call of the Spirit again and again and think that there will always be another chance for them. The world is filled with lost people who are walking the streets of their cities and towns, people who will never be in the bride of Christ because they turned away from the calling of the Spirit too long.

The invitation to come goes out in Matthew 22:2-3. "The kingdom of heaven is like unto a certain king, which made a marriage for his son, and sent forth his servants to call them that were bidden to the wedding; and they would not come." Here we see the Father, speaking about the wedding of His Son, the marriage supper of the Lamb. Those who heard the invitation to the wedding were too busy. They made light of the invitation and gave excuses (verse 5). They despitefully abused those who brought the invitation (verse 6), even killing some of them.

The king, the Father, became very angry and destroyed them and then sent His servants out into the highways and bid the people there to come to the wedding. All around the world today in simple Gospel services in churches large and small, in every type of circumstance, the message is still going forth, "The Father bids you to come to the feast. He wishes a bride for His Son, will you be a part?"

117

The purpose of your invitation to become a faithful child of God is so much greater than just a promise of being delivered from an eternity in hell. Your invitation is to become a part of the very bride of Christ. You have the revealed Word of God for understanding and the guidance and direction of the Holy Spirit that you might fully comprehend and see what is going on both in the natural world and in the spiritual world. You can choose to be tested, refined and adorned in preparation for the marriage supper of the Lamb or you can choose to make an excuse and be put aside.

I do not believe that all who are washed in the blood of Christ are going to be a part of the bride. Search the Scriptures and you will find that there are those who will enter into heaven as by fire. There will be those who are only wedding "guests" who will be present also.

You will notice in this rich parable that there also came one into the wedding (which is referring to the marriage supper of the Lamb and the bride of Christ) who did not have on a wedding garment. His not wearing a wedding garment speaks of the tragedy of those who do not understand the dispensation of the grace and the working of the Holy Spirit today. The Gospel is being preached to the ends of the earth today and multitudes are being born again… but there are still untold thousands who have heard and are convinced, but not converted. You cannot have a wedding garment to put on without a conversion… believing and being convinced will not be enough.

We have churches today filled with people who "believe," but who are not born again—they are convinced but not converted. It is evident by this parable that the New Testament writers foresaw individuals who would name the name of Jesus, be members of churches, serve in the ministry and proclaim God's Word—but who would never enter in to be truly born again. The Word of God says that the bride will be in the image and likeness of the Son of God which can only occur through the new birth. The bride will be presented to her groom fully adorned in her wedding apparel without spot or wrinkle or blemish, conformed to His image and likeness.

There are many who are cleansed, washed in the blood and saved who will just make it inside the doors of heaven to watch the wedding procession as Jesus takes His bride unto Himself. This is clear when we read

1 Corinthians 3:13-15, "Every man's work shall be made manifest: for the day shall declare it, because it shall be revealed by fire; and the fire shall try every man's work of what sort it is. If any man's work abide which he hath built thereupon, he shall receive a reward. If any man's work shall be burned, he shall suffer loss: but he himself shall be saved; yet so as by fire."

The previous passage of Scripture shows the refining process of God. You can be saved, but your works shall reveal what you are in Christ, how much of Jesus has been revealed to you, the depth of your commitment to Him and how much of His life has been able to flow out through you. In 2 Timothy 2:19-20 Paul says, "Nevertheless the foundation of God standeth sure, having this seal, The Lord knoweth them that are his. And, let every one that nameth the name of Christ depart from iniquity. But in a great house there are not only vessels of gold and silver, but also of wood and of earth; and some to honour and some to dishonour." God is speaking here of vessels of common use as compared to those who have entered into a greater manifestation of God to become surrendered vessels that project God by the life they live.

This passage in 2 Timothy 2 should be of real encouragement to every Christian as it explains the possibilities in this great house called the Church. In the body of Christ, there are vessels of gold and of silver. In contrast, there are also some of wood and of earth. Some vessels are for honour and some are for dishonour, or for "common use." In other words, there are some Christians who stir up the love of God by bringing themselves closer to Him through their yieldedness to Him. Each one has the opportunity, by the work of the Holy Spirit in their lives, to be purged of the things that would keep them from being a vessel of honour or of greater use. Each one has the opportunity to be separated from the old patterns and ways that would hinder them so that they could be of greater use to the Master. God is constantly trying to lift us out of the ordinary into the extraordinary by His continual working upon us, in us and through us.

Paul then says in verse 21 of 2 Timothy 2, "If a man therefore purge himself from these (old ways and ignoble use [NIV]), he shall be a vessel unto honour, sanctified, and meet for the master's use, and prepared unto every good work." Paul follows this verse with the urging that all would see that the patterns of their life be changed to live in conformity with God's will.

The Holy Spirit is at work in every Christian, pursuing and pushing, convicting and cleansing, drawing them into refinement for we are the workmanship of the master potter, the Most High God Himself. He takes us out of the world by the new birth and then turns us over to the Holy Spirit that Christ might be revealed within us. Then God fills us with Himself that we would have an unction and an anointing, the power to become adorned for marriage to the Lamb. No loving and adoring bride would ever come to her wedding day until she was properly cleansed, anointed with sweet fragrance, wearing beautiful garments and adorned to be pleasing and desirable to her groom (2 Peter 3:14, Ephesians 5:26-27).

THE PRODIGAL AND THE POTTER

In the parable of the prodigal son, the father provided everything for his two sons that was necessary for life, joy and fulfillment. But one son was not satisfied. Instead of living in contentment, he asked for his portion of all that his father had, his inheritance, and he went off and spent it on riotous living. The father knew that this son was of no use to either himself or to his father as long as he was consumed with self-motivation. So he allowed the son to leave and go out into the world until he came to the end of himself. This is what God does with us sometimes in the dealings of our life. He will give us exactly what we think we have to have and when we have spent our "blessing," we find ourselves alone and without any meaning to our life.

Have you ever found yourself with your back up against the wall or your feet mired down in the pig pen? When this happens, often God has let you live on your self-motivations and desires just as long as it took to get your attention and then He jerked the rug out from under you. Why? So you would cast yourself at His feet as clay. It is then that He can pick you up and begin to shape and mold you into the son or daughter that He knows you can become.

These dealings come in many manners. One example from the Old Testament is the potter and the clay. The clay is dug from the dirt and mixed with water. Then the potter lifts it high and dashes it down on his bench. He takes a wooden paddle and begins to whack that clay, beating air out of it. He beats it and pushes it and pulls it apart, he throws it down on the bench again and again. If the clay could talk (and we do), it would cry out, "You're killing me! What are you doing to me? I can't stand it anymore. You've got to stop! I can't take anymore." Does any of that sound familiar?

After the potter works that clay into a manageable pliability and consistency, he begins to shape it into a vessel. It is one thing to be a chunk of clay and quite another thing to be a vessel. It is one thing to be a rough nugget of gold that needs to be refined and quite another to be a finished vessel of purest gold with a use and a purpose. That is exactly what God does with His children; He shapes, pressures, refines and tests them in their faith so they are ready for His use and His purposes.

Through trials, the testing and all of the growing pains we go through as a Christian, God has us on His potter's wheel. He is making and adorning us as a bride fashioned into the likeness that He wants, vessels fit for the Master's use.

He is forming and making us as in 1 Peter 3:3-4, "Whose adorning let it not be that outward adorning of plaiting the hair, and of wearing of gold, or of putting on of apparel (speaking of outward things), but let it be the hidden man of the heart, in that which is not corruptible, even the ornament of a meek and quiet spirit, which is in the sight of God of great price."

There is a building and a forming going on inside of each one of us that is the making of our hidden spiritual man. We may look into each other's faces, but we cannot see the real person being formed except with our spiritual eyes.

The bride is going to be made up of those who have their inward man adorned by the very graces of Jesus Christ. We will be stepping out of our natural bodies when we meet Him and our spiritual man is the one who will occupy our resurrected bodies. It is our spiritual man who will spend eternity with Jesus. This is the "man" we need to cleanse and clothe with the attributes of Jesus by the washing of the Word and the anointing of prayer.

THE FRAGRANCE OF THE NEW NATURE

The working of grace in our life is constant and ongoing because before the true Church can be raptured, the bride has to be brought into a oneness of language with the Spirit, into conformity with the Holy Spirit as spoken of in the last chapter of the book of Revelation. God is always dealing with us working to break up the hardness and the resistance of our natures, so that the sweetness of the life and nature of Jesus can flow out to the world around us. The Song of Solomon is very descriptive in illustrating the reality of the relationship of the Church's love for Christ and His love for the Church.

The Holy Spirit is working every minute of every day that is left to heal the Church's deformities, purify its motives and bring its actions into the many deep expressions of love—not only from the Church to Jesus, but from one to another.

The Song of Solomon 1:3 says, "Because of the savour of thy good ointments thy name is as ointment poured forth, therefore do the virgins love thee." When the adorning of the bride reaches a certain point that she truly knows exactly who she is, the name of Jesus becomes as sweet smelling oil poured forth to her. His name becomes the only source of satisfaction to her cry for her bridegroom; it becomes a fountain of fragrance in this world we live in.

Jesus was anointed twice in the Scriptures. The first time was when the alabaster box of perfume was broken and poured out upon Him. The second time was when His body was broken and He cried out, "It is finished," and the Holy Spirit was poured forth. When the love and the beauty of Jesus Christ, administered by the Holy Spirit, adorn the spirit of a man or a woman, there is a fragrance that is irresistible to the lost and the unsaved who do not know Him.

Jesus is adorning His bride and He is dealing with all of us through blessings and through testing, as He brings us to decisions of complete obedience and surrender. He is bringing us to the place where we will trust Him in every circumstance. He is fashioning us into the likeness and image of His Son.

In Revelation 3:17, Jesus is speaking of natural adornings, "Because thou sayest, I am rich, and increased with goods, and have need of nothing; and knowest not that thou art wretched, and miserable, and poor and blind, and naked…" Jesus is speaking to the Church, to the believer who has heard the Gospel year in and year out but has not pursued the adorning of their inner man. He is telling them that they are spiritually naked, blind and poor because they have been leaning upon natural things.

Then the Spirit of God speaks to the church of Laodicea, which represents the Church in the last days before the rapture, and counsels her, "…Buy of me gold tried in the fire, that thou mayest be rich; and white raiment, that thou mayest be clothed, and that the shame of thy nakedness do not appear; and anoint thine eyes with eyesalve, that thou mayest see. As many as I love, I rebuke and chasten; be zealous therefore and repent. Behold, I stand at the door and knock; if any man hear my voice, and open the door, I will come in to him, and will sup with him, and he with me" (Revelation 3:18-20).

The Gospel has been preached for nearly 2,000 years. Some have listened, some have started and turned back, some have counted it of no value and some have made light of it. Yet out of all the generations since the birth of Christ, God has gathered Himself a people. But it is you and I who are the incredibly fortunate ones who live in the closing hour… we are the pursued generation that will see the coming of the Messiah. Many generations have passed since the birth, crucifixion and resurrection of Christ and all the Scriptural prophecies regarding the last days before His return are now in the final stages of being fulfilled. We stand at the close of the dispensation of grace or as it is sometimes called, the dispensation of the Holy Spirit. It is to be closed by the gathering out of all those who have made themselves ready.

THE TRAGEDY OF STOPPING SHORT

The time is here when we must lay aside every hindrance and choose to go all the way with God. There are so many Christians who have professed Christ, but who have never entered fully into a relationship with Him. Too many Christians do not realize that there will be millions of people in the tribulation who have heard the Gospel, who can quote the Word and who have professed to believe in Christ, but who have never yielded and surrendered themselves to be a part of His bride. They tragically held back part of themselves in order that they could enjoy some of their earthly comforts and ties to the world.

It is so sad when one does not go far enough in God. In Genesis 11:31, "Terah took Abram his son, and Lot the son of Haran his son's son, and Sarai his daughter-in-law, his son Abram's wife; and they went forth with them from Ur of the Chaldees to go into the land of Canaan; and they came unto Haran, and dwelt there."

They all started out from Ur of the Chaldees and headed for Canaan, but they stopped at Haran (the halfway point) and dwelt there. But only two verses later (at the beginning of the twelfth chapter) the Lord said to Abram, "Get thee out of thy country, and from thy kindred, and from thy father's house, unto a land that I will shew thee. And I will make of thee a great nation, and I will bless thee, and make thy name great; and thou shalt be a blessing. And I will bless them that bless thee, and curse him that curseth thee; and in thee shall all families of the earth be blessed" (Genesis 12:1-3).

This family had come halfway to the land of Canaan and they stopped to rest in a beautiful, green valley. Terah was old and he was probably very tired, so he must have decided it would be a good idea not to go on any further. So he stayed. But in the next two verses, God said to Abram, "Don't stop here, don't fall short, go on all the way. If you will go on, I will give you a promise. It will cost you many things, it will cost you your parents, it will cost you struggle and tears; but if you go on, I will bless you. I will bless those who bless you and I will bless your future household which will be as the sands of the sea."

The world is full of men and women, young and old, who are reaping tears today because they stopped halfway. There are so many "arks" that have only been half-built and are unable to stand the storms that are raging upon the face of the earth. Jesus did not only indwell you so you would be lifted out of your sin, but He indwells you so that your spiritual house will be built strong and sturdy upon the rock. And when the storms come and the rains descend, your house will stand through the apostasy, the evil times and all the works of the devil unleashed upon the world in these end times.

There are no deficits in His grace; there is no weakness in His plan. The weakness occurs when we stop at the halfway house or when we are "almost there and that seems to be close enough." When we stop short and put down roots where we are not supposed to, we do not complete the plan that God has for our life and we end up settling for second best or sometimes something much worse.

Many of our problems today are because we have not gone far enough. We became side-tracked, intimidated and when things pressed in hard upon us, we felt justified in not going any further.

I remember reading a story when I was a boy about a man who had been prospecting for gold in another country. He spent all he had, suffered the cold, worked diligently and tried to gather in the riches like others seemed to be doing. Finally he gave up in frustration and said, "What's the use?" He went back home to the States and left the mine he had started. The mine lay dormant for a long time and eventually the processes of law established the right of another man to take it over. In less than twenty-four hours of hard work, that new owner struck the richest vein of gold ever found in that area. The first owner gave up just twenty-four hours away from moving far enough into the incredible riches of that mine.

I remember another true story of a man who was drilling for oil in an area where oil was plentiful, but all he turned up was dry holes. Finally, he gave up and another man took over. After drilling for a few days, the new man brought in gushers of oil and became very wealthy. The first man gave up too soon.

This reminds me of some of our Pentecostal people. They will pray and seek God with all of their hearts and then they give up before the "oil" comes in. They try again and give up again. They go somewhere else and give it their all, but give up again. If they would only stay down on their knees long enough, they would strike oil and uncover gleaming veins of gold. But they keep stopping just short of the victory.

READING THE ROAD SIGNS

We must always remember that we are just pilgrims in this land, our real dwelling place is not here on earth. We are only passing through as we move towards home. The minute that we begin to root down and dig in, the moment we begin to give up and not push on any farther, that is the time when we begin to conform to this world. The building of the spiritual man within us slows down and finally stops.

Everything in this world is designed to sidetrack us from our ultimate objective as a Christian and to confuse our identity as a child of God. Satan is ingenious with his distractions and temptations, often cleverly disguising them as "opportunities" for further growth or an unusual avenue of working for the Lord. We must always be spiritually sensitive to the detecting of his subtle works in our life, for it is relatively easy for most sincere believers to recognize the obvious ones. Don't be a Christian who is satisfied with shallow victories, spiritual status quo and surface blessings for the Holy Spirit wants to take you deeper into the realm of being a true overcomer.

The Holy Spirit is always faithful to lead and to guide us, but we must be aware and watching for the road signs along the way. We must know that turns and twists in the road are sometimes the Holy Spirit's way of teaching us a keener sense of balance and sharper driving "skills". If you see a spiritual "guard rail," stay away from it for there is a potential drop-off on the other side of it. If you see a "double white line," know that you should be careful to stay in your own lane at this time.

When you find yourself on a spiritual freeway and some Christians are dragging along in the slow lane in front of you, follow the Holy Spirit's leading to move out into the fast lane to "get on down the road." Take care that you do not become engrossed with the world's billboards along the way or the brightly lit off ramps of the devil. Always stay in direct communication with your guide, the Holy Spirit, and pull in to water and refuel only at His "rest stops."

THE PRICE OF LOOKING BACK

You must remember that your promises from God did not come to you through Abraham's parents who stopped halfway; they came to you through Abraham who went all the way with God. After Abraham left the others and went on, the rest of the family who stayed at Haran probably thought they had it pretty good. The water was running freely, the crops were good and the pasture was fertile. The cattle and the sheep began to multiply. Men and women can be fooled, when they are prospering materially, into thinking that God is smiling on them and blessing them because they have gone far enough with Him.

Abraham went on into some rough circumstances. Following God had caused him to lose some of his family and he also probably had to give up some of the family possessions that they had been jointly using while they were all together. He was lonely and afraid at times. There is a truth here that is hard for many people to receive—you do not move deeper into a relationship with God while you are in a crowd. God has to get you alone before He can reveal a fuller understanding of His purposes for your life and His deeper truths to you. It was when Abraham went on alone, all the way, that the great promises of God for the whole human race came to pass through him.

Lot, Abraham's nephew, went on and made it past the halfway point of Haran, but then he settled into Sodom—an unfortunate choice that nearly cost him his life. It did cost him the lives of his wife and most of his family. Lot knew the Lord and His salvation, but he lost his testimony. He entered into the pattern of Sodom, becoming a full citizen of Sodom which was a type of the world. He lost his testimony and could not affect any of his sons-in-law or his married daughters with his pleadings to flee the city before God's wrath descended upon it. Because his life seemed to be no different than theirs, they saw no reason why they should listen to him and they mocked him and turned away from his words of warning.

When the angels were ready to depart from Sodom on the morning of the great disaster descending upon it, even then Lot lingered and they had to pull him, his wife and his two daughters out of the city. Against their warnings, Lot's wife looked back and was immediately turned into a pillar of salt. Lot and his two daughters were spared, but everyone else was destroyed. Lot's life continued to be filled with tragedy as he lived in a cave with his daughters, descending to drunkenness and incest as related in Genesis 19. His life continued to spiral downward because he had not gone far enough with God.

It is important to realize that our families, our neighbours and our unsaved friends will never listen to us if we have lost our testimony as Lot did. When we try to tell them of the impending doom of the end times which are near at hand, they will laugh and mock us openly or behind our backs.

There are Christians who believe that they can play around and make compromises with the world, taking their Christian experience lightly, and then one day move on into a deeper walk with God once they have satisfied their carnal yearnings. Sin and carnality always leave deep scars, especially the sin and carnality of the Christian who is leading a double life. This person can eventually acquire a seared conscience that no longer bothers them. They ultimately can reach a point where they truly don't care anymore.

They might have one last opportunity to restore their position with God upon a deathbed experience of repentance and regret or they may depart this earth without ever having been able to repent and make things right. Their final resting in eternity will be a dreadful one. But the greater tragedy still will be all of their friends and family members who learned to despise and reject Christ because of the double standards and hypocrisy in their life.

God is a God of forgiveness, yes, but the carnal Christians who have played around with the world will suffer from the wounds of a worldly life when they seek to once again find the sweetness of a pure relationship with Jesus. Jesus does not hold back, for He always stands with open arms to bring a lost sheep back into the fold. But there are slow-to-heal wounds, jagged scars and broken places within the Christian who has indulged himself in the world that Satan will viciously attack again and again. Backslidden Christians who return to the arms of the Saviour may struggle desperately in their battle to overcome the memories and torments of what the enemy wrought in their lives during the time when they walked away from God. We must show unconditional love and support both in person and in prayer for any Christian who has come back to God. Their steps back are often very painful ones and they need all of the encouragement and acceptance that we can give.

The man or the woman who does not go far enough with God will pay with tears and regret. They may pay for their stubbornness or their apathy in refusing to go all the way with the lost souls of loved ones. They may pay for it with rebellious, wilful children. There is no pain quite like the pain of seeing your own children paying the price for your wilfulness.

PARALLEL TRUTHS:
THE STRENGTH AND MIGHT OF TINY ISRAEL
THE LIFE OF THE CHRISTIAN TODAY

One of the final happenings to come to pass before the return of our Lord is that when the armies begin to encompass Israel, the desolation thereof is nigh (Luke 21:20). When this occurs, these will be the final days when all things which have been written in the Scriptures will come to fulfillment (Luke 21:22). As we look at Israel today, the armies are moving in on her.

Israel stands out as God's time clock in this present hour when we see the rising of the Arab world and the coming together of powerful forces against the Jews. Even at this hour, new approaches are being made to the Arab world and the strength of the Arabs is rising as they battle to retake some of the territory that belongs to Israel, especially the Golan Heights. Even though the Arabs and the Jews are half-brothers, they are the conflicting forces through which God's Word is going to be fulfilled.

The reason that Israel is so strong, as it repels all attacks against it, is that it is surrounded by enemies. Tiny Israel is mighty because it knows that it must resist the forces around it, its very survival depends upon being strong on every front. Its strength has been built by its determined resistance to its enemies.

There is a parallel here in our Christian life that we must always remember. Your strength of character is not being formed in heaven—it is being formed right here! It takes resistance to build true Christian character. Our strength comes from character that has been built by consistently resisting the forces of evil that are all around us. We are living in a devastating world that has one determination in mind and that is to destroy the true character of the body of Christ and bring it into bondage and disharmony with God. These very forces of evil are the factors by which we build our Christian character as we stand in resistance to them.

MOVING IN GOD'S PERFECT TIMING

Abraham had received a promise from God that He would bless him and that his descendants would be as the sands of the sea and the stars of the heaven. Abraham walked with God and trusted Him, but as the years kept rolling by, Abraham began to wonder if God had forgotten him. He began to question God in his heart as to where was the son who would bring forth his future descendants.

As he began to doubt and waiver in unbelief, he transgressed the plan of God and decided that he had to help God with the fulfillment of His promise. Sarah faltered in her faith as well. She suggested that he go in unto her Egyptian maid, Hagar, and have a child since Sarah believed she was too far past the age of childbearing. Scripture says that Abraham didn't hesitate, but that "he hearkened to the voice of Sarah... and he went in unto Hagar and she conceived" (Genesis 15:2, 4). Here is a perfect picture of us when God is not moving according to our time schedule and we decide that we had better do something to get things going. Just like Abraham, we end up creating many of our own problems.

Abraham had a son by Hagar named Ishmael. Abraham moved out of God's will and produced the son that he thought would be the son of promise. But the son of promise, Isaac, came through Sarah just like God had said he would. Ishmael was the son of the flesh, the son of carnality and disobedience. Abraham became the father of Ishmael, but Isaac was the son of the promise. The Arabs still claim that they are the sons of promise and the hate and the battle mounts, constantly fanned by Satan himself. Ishmael and his descendants have been in conflict with Israel throughout history and it will not stop until the end of time when Jesus returns... this is a type of the carnal nature of man warring endlessly with the spiritual man.

The storm clouds of tribulation are mounting and mankind is reaching a point of great consternation and fear. But the Church should be rejoicing and gearing up for the final harvest, for the fig tree is budding and the time of His return is near. We are in the final days of our preparation, the final days of searching our hearts and surrendering our ties to the world. It is a day of strengthening our vows, intensifying our prayer life and seeking God with all our hearts.

The bride of Christ and the Spirit are moving into the unity where they can say together, "Come, Lord Jesus." We must be certain that we are sensitive to the Spirit's voice, that we can hear Him at all times. We must be in control of our environment so that our sensitivity to the Spirit is undistracted. We create a spiritual environment around us by prayer, by taking authority over Satan's distractions and by the washing of the Word. We spiritually discern any intrusions of the enemy and reject them.

The Church is waiting right now, not for another love letter from God, not for more gifts and blessings, but for the personal return of the Lord Jesus Himself. The Holy Spirit is waiting for the Church to be completed and to come together in unity with Him to say, "Come, Lord Jesus."

CHAPTER 8

THE SPIRIT AND THE BRIDE SAY, "COME"

It is exciting to look at all the verses in the book of Revelation in light of current events as the prophecies of the Word of God are being unveiled in the day in which we live—but it is the following passage of Scripture that is the last and final call of the Spirit to the world.

"I, Jesus have sent mine angel to testify unto you these things in the churches. I am the root and the offspring of David, and the bright and morning star. And the Spirit and the bride say, Come. And let him that heareth say, Come. And let him that is athirst come. And whosoever will, let him take the water of life freely" (Revelation 22:16-17).

Jesus is the root and the offspring of David. He is everything that is fore-shadowed throughout the entire Bible. He is exactly who the prophets said He would be. He is the Alpha and the Omega, the first and the last. He is the one who is going to have the authority to take over the rulership of the whole universe. He is the one who is going to purge the world of its curse and prepare it for the flow of the water of life proceeding out from the throne of God, pure as crystal and without the blight of sin.

In the book of Revelation, Jesus is speaking to the churches that have passed from death unto life. He is telling them that the Spirit and His bride will say together, "Come." The word "come" is a very rich and full word. It is an invitational word. Noah was invited to "come" into the ark and be saved from the flood. Moses, in the midst of the camp, said, "Come, and stand by me." The book of Isaiah says, "Come, let us reason together."

When the Spirit and the bride finally can say in unity, "Come," it will mean that everything is ready and in waiting. Jesus will not come back until complete harmony has been reached between His bride-to-be and Himself. The bride of Christ, now in preparation through the workings of the Spirit, has to be brought to a certain level of readiness and harmony before Jesus can come again.

When the lambs begin to bleat, their shepherd will come. We are His lambs and we are bleating, but what are we bleating for? Too many of us are still holding onto our dreams, our plans, our longings and our desires, and these are uppermost in our cries unto Him. Before Jesus comes again, however, the true Church will have to come to a place where there is nothing that is more important to it than His coming. The lambs will have such a homesickness for the coming of Jesus that they will cry out for nothing else. The spirit of the bride of Christ will have such a yearning for His coming that every Christian will arise each morning and say, "Jesus, are you coming today?"

I remember calling my grandson Davey on the telephone when he was very young and, upon hearing me on the line, he cried out, "I've been waiting for you!" What love is expressed in that excited exclamation; "I've been waiting for you!" The bride is coming to a final fulfillment where she can cry out in unity to Jesus, "I am ready, please come, I have been waiting for you!"

There is a fine tuning going on in the body of Christ and the world right now. The universe, the world and time itself were all made for the Son of God, but when sin came into the world, everything fell out of harmony. Sin put the sting in the mosquito bite, the roar into the lion and the anger into the bear. Sin is the key to the churning, angry waters of man and nature.

In this very hour, all creation is groaning to be delivered of its past. God's greatest creation, mankind, is groaning to be delivered of its body.

What is He doing right now with His children who have been made clean and who have received the implantation of His life? What is the fine tuning that the Spirit is doing? He is helping us to loosen our grip upon this world, to let go until the world becomes only our servant and not our master.

Our spirits are crying, "Jesus, come quickly!" When will He come? When the Spirit and the bride are one in unity. The Holy Spirit is at work in the bride, bringing her to a place where she can speak like the Spirit. If you haven't yet been able to hear what the Spirit is saying to the Church, He is trying to knock at your door right now so that the Spirit and the bride will have one voice. Every circumstance in our life is related to bringing us into harmony with what God is doing in the world as well as within the lives of men and women who are moving with Him. He is not willing that anyone should be lost and He is dealing with those who are out of relationship with Him as well as those who are in relationship with Him.

To those of us who are doing our best to move with God, the Holy Spirit is bringing us to the highest spiritual level that He can. This is the day when God is speaking strongly to the Church so that all will be ready. The Spirit is crying out the message that time is drawing very near to the end. As we feel and hear that cry, recognizing what He is saying, we must make ourselves ready.

The work of the Holy Spirit is to perfect, lead, guide, deal with, direct and press the Church into the fullness of who Christ is. The body of Christ is now being scrubbed clean, washed by the water of His Word. Our minds are being washed, our emotions are being washed, our attitudes are being washed and He will continue washing us until we are sanctified. He is cleansing our motives, our desires and our ambitions until we completely surrender them to the greater life of His purpose within us.

THE TREE OF LIFE

The Holy Spirit closes the book of Revelation with triumph as He ends this portion of the written Word in a glorious climax of truth. He reminds us of certain things and then He blesses us by saying that there is going to be a healing of all things. The leaves of the Tree of Life are for the healing of the nations. The first three verses of the final chapter of the book of Revelation tell us, "And he shewed me a pure river of water of life, clear as crystal, proceeding out of the throne of God and of the Lamb. In the midst of the street of it, and on either side of the river, was there the tree of life, which bare twelve manner of fruits, and yielded her fruit every month: and the leaves of the tree were for the healing of the nations. And there shall be no more curses; but the throne of God and of the Lamb shall be in it; and his servants shall serve him."

Notice that there are two things mentioned very clearly here. First, there is the Tree of Life which is first mentioned in the book of Genesis. God spoke to Adam and Eve about two trees, one was the Tree of Knowledge of good and evil and the other tree was the Tree of Life. He said that they could partake of the Tree of Life, but the Tree of Knowledge was forbidden to them. If they would have partaken of that Tree of Life, they would have lived forever.

The Tree of Life represented the very life of God—life emanating from a discernable object that they could see with their natural eyes. If they had been obedient and only partaken of the Tree of Life, they would have been blessed by God and all that He had to offer them. The untested life within Adam and Eve was being tested by choices.

That same tree surfaces again and again as the life stream runs through the Old and the New Testament, climaxing in the final chapter of the book of Revelation. "And the fruit of that tree (speaking of the leaves) are for the healing of the nations." What is going to be the healing of the nations? The life of God going forth from the body of those who shall be in that glorious rapture and the return of Christ when He comes to rule and reign. Besides the healing of the nations, there shall be no more curses which have been upon all nature and all nations. The blessings of the life stream of God will flow through every part of His creation from the trees of the field and the animals of the woods to the very nature of man.

THE APOSTLE JOHN ALONE WITH GOD

A few years ago, it was my privilege to stand amid the ruins outside of Ephesus near the grave and tomb of the Apostle John. As I looked out over his grave across the Aegean Sea, I wondered about the Isle of Patmos some thirty miles away where John was banished for a period of time.

I could imagine the aging apostle, perhaps with a long, grey beard, whose only crime was that he had shared too much of Jesus with those who lived around him. He was uncontrollable in this aspect and this was too great an offence for the emperor of Rome. The emperor didn't kill John because he feared the reaction of the people, but he determined he could get away with banishing John to the Isle of Patmos to die from starvation or old age.

But God had another plan. John did not know that when the emperor exiled him to the Isle of Patmos that God only wanted a man taken away from the rest of the world. As John was shut off by himself in a seemingly ungodly circumstance, God began to unveil the greatest revelation ever made to a mortal mind. God has to put some of us into an isolated situation before He can fully have our attention to tell us certain things. It is interesting to speculate that John might have been so zealous in his work of evangelism and spreading the Gospel that God had to slow him down and hold him steady while He revealed the mysteries and the glory of the book of Revelation to him.

Out of the secret chambers of the Father's heart, through the Son by the Holy Spirit, John received a sweeping view of future events while on the Isle of Patmos.

John was far too submerged in God to be threatened by anything man could throw at him and he had gone too far with the truth to ever backtrack. He had enough revelation of the Father and the Son that he cared nothing about his own life. I believe that John's words and feelings would have been similar to this, "I have found the answer and if I don't live any longer, what difference does it make? I am anxious to get home anyway. The revelation of Jesus is like a fire burning within my bones and I cannot contain it. The world shall know who He is because the Christ that they crucified has built His kingdom within my heart. Though I walk the soil of this earth in human flesh, the King of heaven on earth is within me and I cannot hold it back. This world shall know who the resurrected Christ really is!"

His unquenchable desire to share the revelation of Christ was John's "problem," this is what put him on the Isle of Patmos. It was there that he began to record what he saw through the telescope of time and eternal truth began to explode within him. He began to see what was going to happen. He saw the preaching of the Gospel... he saw the gathering of the nations and the people from the different countries of the world. He saw the religious truths and the patterns that would come. He revealed this to the seven churches in his writings, but they did not have an ear to hear what the Spirit said unto them.

In the closing chapter of the book of Revelation, John makes a final appeal directly from Jesus Himself, "I have sent an angel to share these things with the churches, so let them hear."

The Gospel was implanted into the early Church, the seven churches of the book of Revelation. But they became too busy doing things their own way and they returned to making the rounds of their traditions. They were sharing the Gospel, but compromising it as they saw it and felt it. Jesus had a message for them, but they couldn't receive it because they did not have ears to hear. They were not listening to Him, so He sent His beloved John with the message again. Most of them didn't listen to him either. I believe that you and I are in the last generation that will have an opportunity to hear His call.

A GENERATION PURSUED

We are a pursued generation. God Himself is pursuing us. He has waited for this since the beginning of time, a generation marked as being different from any other. James 5:7 says, "...Behold the husbandman waiteth for the precious fruit of the earth and has long patience for it..."

This generation which you and I live in is the generation spoken of that would see Israel become a nation again as it finally did in 1948. This is the generation that would watch Jerusalem cease to be trodden under by the Gentiles when Israel took it back after nearly 2,000 years.

It is the generation that will see the Jew come from the east and the west and the north and the south as spoken of in Isaiah 43:5-6, "Fear not; for I am with thee. I will bring thy seed from the east, and gather thee from the west. I will say to the north, Give up; and to the south, Keep not back. Bring my sons from far and my daughters from the ends of the earth." God said to the nations that had held them captive, "Let them go!"

We are the generation which has seen all of these things begin to happen... the generation that faces what seems to be a no-win situation through the circumstances in the world with wars, bombs and missiles, terrorists, epidemics of killer viruses, rampant crime, drug abuse and the other perplexities of the day.

We have finally arrived, for we are the "X" generation! God has long waited with patience for this harvest. History is envious of this generation. The prophets envisioned it, the apostles preached towards it, the disciples foretold it, Jesus proclaimed it, our forefather's died for it and you and I were born into it!

Hear what the Spirit is trying to say to this generation. There are things in the heavens and in the earth that are in great change and transition. God has released the hungering spirits of man to search for the revelation of a life to be lived in Him. Those who do not turn to God will destroy themselves trying to quench the despair and hunger that burns within them. This root of despair has invaded the religious world as men and women began to find out that their doctrines have not become experience; their beliefs have not turned into reality.

The Holy Spirit is not going to let God's people be mediocre, half-hearted or just bleacher warmers. He is not going to let you watch "someone else do it." He is going to put a hunger inside of each one of us that will drive us to distraction until we lay hold of His life breaking forth in our spirit.

Even if we begin to question things we know to be true, that will only drive us to our knees and deeper into the Word to confirm their truth.

God is bringing multitudes of men and women to a point where they realize that the only real life is in Him. It is not our life properly disciplined and taught, but it is His life that will rise up in us in order that we can be who God wants us to be. Our generation is experiencing a hunger that will press some into a corner, a hunger that will drive many to spend all night long searching the Scriptures. This hunger will bring some to spend all day on their knees as God works to fully form His life on the inside of them.

The womb of this generation holds the completion of the ages and will give forth the birth of the full revelation of the King of Kings, the Lord of Lords, and His return. This is what the body of Christ is collectively carrying within itself. The true body of Christ from around the world will give birth to the unveiling of the completion of the ages in the return of the Lord Jesus. The fig tree is budding and putting forth its leaves and we need to recognize that the time is very near; it is even at the door.

THE EVIL ONE IS IN PURSUIT TOO

Not only is this generation pursued by God, it is being pursued by Satan as well. This generation is the target of hell more than any other generation since Jesus' day. The enemy is going to try to accentuate every weakness he can find, he is going to try to divide every home and destroy every life. There is nothing to fear, however, as long as the Christian stays close to Jesus because He knows every single thing that Satan is doing every second. As long as your eyes are on Christ, God will only allow those things to happen to you that are going to continue to work out His purpose in your life.

Satan has done everything he has been able to think of since the outpouring of the Holy Spirit to sidetrack, pervert, confuse and bury the Gospel in order to create doubt. He has worked feverishly to prevent men and women from going far enough in their faith to receive a real revelation of Christ and the plan of God for their lives. Satan tried to entrap Jesus and His followers, but Jesus defeated him and a new, victorious life was humanized within Jesus' own body... the life of the Father in the Son which is now in the believer. Jesus, through His life, death, resurrection and the acceptance by the Father of His sacrifice, prepared an incorruptible seed to be planted into the spirits of mankind.

Jesus came to plant that perfected seed of new life into the spirits of men and women who were eternally lost. He has caused it to germinate, to sprout and to be watered by the Word. He has brought maturity to the seed through the work of the Holy Spirit and He has caused it to take root inside of each one of us who have determined to believe in Him. His ultimate purpose is to see it grow into a strong spiritual man inside of each one of us.

This generation needs to see themselves as the Lord sees them. Do you have your identification right as a member of the body of Christ? I'm not just an ordinary person and neither are you, nor is any other Christian. You are a son or a daughter of God. The very life of eternity is in your spiritual veins. You were created in His image for His purpose to be the channels of His power. When we begin to finally see who we really are and the bride comes into the unity of spirit and purpose that God has ordained, THEN JESUS WILL COME.

THE WORK TO BE DONE

The Holy Spirit has brought forth the revelation of Christ to you and me in order that we will be clothed in the fullness of Jesus' likeness before we leave this world. God is going to deal with and pull out every bitter root growing within the lives of His children. He is going to purify every motive and remove every animosity within us because we, the bride of Christ, and the Spirit are going to be one. This is the hour and the generation of the fulfillment of the adorning of the bride and the Holy Spirit is revealing Jesus to us in such a way as never before. The Spirit is bringing us into harmony with Jesus so that He and the bride can say, "Come!" Don't be a Christian who only cries out to Jesus to come when you are in trouble. Then, when you are out of the trouble, you secretly say in your heart, "Jesus... everything is okay now, could you please wait just a little longer." God might have to keep you perpetually in trouble to keep you crying out in harmony with the other members of the body of Christ, "Come quickly, Lord Jesus."

The bride of Christ and the Spirit must be in unity, working together and speaking together as one in these final days. God has established His pattern and the bride and the Spirit must cooperate together to complete it. The Holy Spirit has full power to enlighten men's minds, awaken their spirits and move upon their emotions to bring them into submission from their rebellion against God. Yet He works only within the plan of God and God has decreed that the bride of Christ must intercede and travail for the lost souls of the world. If the bride fails to intercede, the Holy Spirit cannot do His work of convicting and persuading.

The Spirit and the bride must work and travail together for souls to be saved. If the bride does not travail, the Spirit will not move. The first words of the bride today should be, "Lord, release your Spirit to the convicting work of sin and crush every resistance of those who have failed to respond."

One of the most powerful factions within the bride of Christ in these end times is the dear and precious older saints, the proven prayer warriors who get down regularly on their knees and travail for lost souls. These dear saints, often widows and widowers, who sometimes feel they have nothing to offer God in this endtime struggle, are actually storming against the chains of hell itself.

Perhaps it is well that they will only find out in heaven as to how many prison doors opened and how many chains fell off as a result of their prayer life; they will probably almost have a heart attack when they realize the magnitude of the work they have accomplished for God through their intercession. God bless these sweet prayer warriors; they are the driving force behind the men and women who suddenly cry out, "What is happening to me? My life is empty, everything is meaningless. What can I do?" In response to these warriors' prayers, the Holy Spirit has removed every source of water these lost souls knew of until there is only one place left for them to go... to Jesus! The Holy Spirit can and will persuade anyone if the Church prevails far enough.

Christian, do you realize how much power over life and death you hold in your hands? It is more than the world's power and it is more than all of the devils in Satan's crowd put together. The Church holds the balance of power not only in world affairs, but in the salvation of the souls of millions.

THIS GENERATION IS REACHING FOR ITS NEW BODY

These old garments of flesh are old and they're breaking down. They have been nourished by sin, disease, bondages and fear handed down for some 6,000 years. Yet they are able to house the resurrection life of the incorruptible seed Himself. The flesh of mankind has been so interlaced with disease and sin and made weak through the processes of time that it seems sickness is breaking out in greater dimensions all over the world than ever before. The medical profession is almost beside itself with such diseases as AIDS and many other virulent viruses that keep defensively rearranging their molecular structure faster than scientists can come up with new drugs to combat them.

As I have ministered in various countries around the world in crusades, I have seen up to ninety percent of those present raise their hands for the healing of their bodies. Human bodies are breaking down and the hospitals are full. America is spending more and more on physical and mental health programs and research than ever before, and we're not winning the race against time with disease.

This old body of flesh is crying out, reaching out for its new body. Only the unveiling of the Christ within us in a greater degree by the Holy Spirit will keep these old bodies walking around a little longer until the rapture takes place. Yet our bodies can refuse this unveiling of Christ within if we allow our soul (which is our mind, will and emotions) to hinder the Holy Spirit's work in us. But even with just a small effort towards God on our part, He will break through the shell that the world and our old nature have tried to place around our spirits. He will break through by using circumstances, trouble and reverses if He has to when we don't reach out to Him on our own. He might even use a spiritual two-by-four.

The Holy Spirit is at work in you and me at all times, whether we're listening or not. You might not believe that this is true in your life for you don't feel you have any joy (peace, love, etc...). That does not matter, for the fruits of the Spirit are still there in you. You do not receive the life of Jesus (containing His attributes which have been tested, proven perfect and are all a part of the incorruptible seed) in chapters or instalments. You receive all of Him, everything He is, in one complete package. Then why aren't you perfect? Because God is not through with you yet.

God, through the Holy Spirit, is constantly working in your life to crumble old resistances, rebellions and walls that are holding back the full release of His life into your spirit. What a treasure we have in these old, earthen vessels! It's been housed in human vessels for 2,000 years since Christ's resurrection. He is within your spirit and mine right now, alive and well. Mankind's old, fleshly frame has become hardened by time and pressure. The motivation within the bodies of the man and woman without God is becoming very dim, but the child of God has the light of Christ within them.

WHEN THE LIGHTS GO OUT

In the story of the five foolish virgins and the five wise virgins, the virgins who were foolish were not harlots, they were not unclean or wicked. They had the same vessels, they all had oil to start with and they all had been brought up with the same training. They were all looking for the same bridegroom with expectancy in their hearts. What caused them to be left outside? They lacked enough motivation to make ample provision for that which was important, the oil for their lamps. They let other things take up their time.

Oil here does not necessarily mean the Holy Spirit, rather in this context it means life. They allowed deterioration in an area of their lives where they should have made ample provision... they should have been prepared. It wasn't necessary that they would run out of oil.

Neither is it necessary that the Church would ever be unprepared. It is not necessary for Christians to go through many of the crises that they do; they only go through them because they have lacked motivation to be properly prepared.

LIVING ON THE EDGE OF TIME

The quest for power and personal empires has become a consuming force in humanity today. Materialism is a highly self-destructive factor in society as men and women are ruining themselves with their habits and their desires. Sex has been flaunted and perverted until it has opened a cesspool that is drowning men, women and innocent children alike in its quagmire. The mystery of iniquity is closing in on this affluent society of the world. The world is being ruled by the spirits of greed, power, lust and all of the other spirits that crawl out of the devil's darkness. People in every nation of the world have tried to overcome the helplessness of their circumstances by anything that can temporarily make the frightening reality of a world out of control go away. The attitude of much of our society ranges from fear to fatalism, from disbelief to depression.

It is said that the lack of motivation in the average American today is one of the great causes of the rising inflation in our economy. Workers from past days produced more in eight hours than they do today. It is not that they have become lazy or incapable, it is because the average American does not have the dreams and the visions that he or she once had. Time is spent today on survival and getting by. Many Americans are just trying to stay ahead of their circumstances.

In addition to decreased motivation and a diminished hope for the future, men and women are battling an inflamed spirit of materialism, self-indulgence and greed. Our great nation is being rocked by the desire for power and money and self-gratification. With the decreased motivation and productivity level now in force, men and women who want increasingly more have begun to look for an easy way to satisfy their desires. This is what has led to the monumental upswing in dishonesty and crime in the world in the last two decades.

There is a deep darkness of the law of sin and death as spoken of in Romans destroying mankind everywhere today because there is a time limit on the amount of sin our bodies can live under. Education that was meant to bring freedom is now bringing bondage. Comforts that were meant to bless have now become economic curses as many are literally strapped to

145

the walls in trying to have what were once considered everyone's due... a home, a car, clothes and recreation.

Most of our water is unfit to drink without chemical purification and much of our air is unhealthy to breathe. There are food shortages everywhere with whole nations in the world starving. Products on our grocer's shelves may now be laced with poison by people with perverted minds. Scientists have read the ticking of the clock towards the midnight hour and everyone in the world knows that something is going to happen soon.

GOD'S PERFECT TIMING

Today's generation wants to be unclothed from the trappings of its humanity, unencumbered from the carnal desires and dealings of men and women. We want to be delivered from our limitations. We want to be delivered from the bondage of a body that is responding to the death notices of this world. There is something stirring on the inside of this pursued generation, both in the saved and unsaved alike.

God has perfect timing for everything. There is a law of deterioration. When you plant a seed in the ground, the outer hull must decay and disintegrate before the life within that seed can germinate and spring forth. Your spirit is vitally alive and straining to get out of the shell of your body (which you have rested your hopes upon in your natural life). It is wanting to spring forth in its new form just like the beautiful stalk of corn comes forth from the tiny, dried up, hard seed of corn that is dropped into the ground.

Jesus is working to help you see that you must allow His life to break forth in your spirit until you realize that life here on earth is just a base camp on the edge of time. Your body is just a space suit for an expedition into the spirit world and a magnificent adventure in the supernatural power of God that is about to be unleashed in a greater magnitude than ever before in our generation. Jesus says that this body will be like a worn out garment that we will shed in His perfect timing.

This world has more than enough pressure to break men and women mentally, physically and spiritually and it is not going to get any better.

146

But while the pressures of the world increase, Jesus just keeps increasing His resurrection life and power within His people… He just turns up the volume and opens the downspout from heaven a little more to release life to His own. As He increases the release of His life and the power of His Word, we will rise above our aging, our finances, our appetites and everything of this world that we have held so dear. It will become a reality in our spirits that Jesus is the absolute center of everything we want and need and desire. That is when He can finally turn His full power and authority loose through us to become supernatural Christians in these end times.

2 Corinthians 4:7-11, "But we have this treasure in earthen vessels, that the excellency of the power may be of God, and not of us. We are troubled on every side, yet not distressed; we are perplexed, but not in despair; persecuted, but not forsaken; cast down, but not destroyed. Always bearing about in the body the dying of the Lord Jesus, that the life also of Jesus might be made manifest in our body. For we which live are always delivered unto death for Jesus' sake, that the life also of Jesus might be made manifest in our mortal flesh."

In order to bring about the release of the provision on the inside of you, there is the law of deterioration and death operating in your life.

OUR SPIRITUAL HOUSE BUILT FROM WITHIN

God has given something to the Christian who is sold out to Him that will be absolutely foreign to all others in the day in which we live. When governors, the presidents, the millionaires and the generals have run out of gas, the Christian who has a hold of the life stream of Jesus Christ will just keep getting stronger every day. Everything in life that does not have His divine life within itself will decay and be destroyed, but the presence of His life will always bring fresh vitality and strength.

God's people will not lose their sense of direction, their spiritual priorities, their anointing from Him or the realities within their spirit. He will take care of His own every step of the way for God is never behind schedule or caught off guard. Every step that mankind makes is moving this generation towards its final hour of destiny… and each Christian in this generation will find themselves with the exact amount of Jesus Christ's resurrection life and power that they have allowed the Holy Spirit to prepare them to be able to contain.

"For we know that if our earthly house of this tabernacle were dissolved, we have a building of God, an house not made with hands, eternal in the heavens. For in this we groan, earnestly desiring to be clothed upon with our house which is from heaven; if so be that being clothed we shall not be found naked. For we that are in this tabernacle do groan, being burdened; not for that we would be unclothed, but clothed upon, that mortality might be swallowed up of life. Now he that hath wrought us for the selfsame thing is God, who also hath given unto us the earnest of the Spirit (2 Corinthians 5:1-5).

While our body is crying out, we sit under the revelation of the Holy Spirit and the Word of God. The life of Jesus Christ (who is the source of all wisdom and knowledge and the center of all things) is constantly being drawn out of His glory by the Holy Spirit and deposited within the spirits of men and women who are alive unto Him. He is building a spiritual house on the inside of each one of us who will let Him. When this spiritual house has reached a certain maturity, it begins to press against the walls of the limitations of our old body. Inside of every earnest Christian is a spiritual man who is standing up and crying out not to be just unclothed from the flesh, but to be clothed upon in the fullness of the eternal plan of God.

When you begin to sense that unveiling of the living Christ within you and you feel the pressure from inside your spirit, let your spirit soar with joy. There are many things you may not understand when your bones creak or your joints crack or reverses and sicknesses come. But the rebuilding of your life and the fulfillment of your purpose in God is going on inside of you and will emerge in all of its fullness. You are still in your old body and you may have trials, doubts, fears and questions. You may not understand many things that are going on around you, but the Spirit is moving in your life anyway. While we are groaning and struggling, there is a new body that is being formed beneath the veil of this flesh, a new tabernacle that is being built.

THE RIVER IS FLOWING

The Holy Spirit has said that the hour has come. We no longer shall listen to the dictates of human desire and to the carnal natures that have flourished under the clothing of religion. The Holy Spirit has opened Ezekiel's river and it is beginning to flow out and it is more than ankle high, it is more than waist high, it is flowing deeper and deeper. The Holy Spirit has poured water into it as it has run through every denomination. It is now water deep enough to swim in. The river is flowing and it is bringing about the healing of every part of Christianity's fractured body of believers today in order to bring about the absolute fullness of the revelation of Jesus within His body before the trumpet sounds.

That new body is in the making and unity in the Spirit is being formed. All over the world, the Spirit of God is breaking loose everywhere. A lot of theologies have had to go down the drain. Many thought that the pouring out of the Holy Spirit in the Charismatic move was a revival of Pentecost. It wasn't and it isn't. The gifts and tongues are only the evidence of the work of the Spirit. We have been given a period in time that has been set aside by God for the work of the Holy Spirit to unveil the mysteries of the revelation of Christ in us which he has kept hidden since the heavens were formed.

SO COME, LORD JESUS

God is doing a mighty work in this generation. How sad it is that He has to run after some of us instead of us running after Him, so that He can teach us and build that spiritual man on the inside of us. But He is going to keep building and working on the bride until she is ready, until the Spirit and the bride are one. Jesus is listening for when the Spirit and the bride say, "Come."

Don't fight or react against what God is doing. Everything that happens to you has a purpose. He's working on you and He always works from the standpoint of eternity, not time as we know it. Don't look for more gifts, don't look for more messages. Look for the unveiling of Christ within you. The Spirit is waiting and Jesus is waiting for the harvest. You're that harvest, plus all of those who died in the faith and all of those who will yet accept Him when they hear the Gospel. When that trumpet finally sounds, the spiritual man will come through and we shall be changed. This old body will fall off and we will have a body like one of the Godhead, a glorified body like Jesus. It will be a body that has been made on the anvil of testing and trial and decisions and faith... cleansed and washed and formed under pressure. The Christian has had to live with all the resistances of this world because resurrection life grows and flourishes against resistance. Character and reality come out of meeting and overcoming obstacles against faith and the nature of a world without God.

2 Corinthians 4 gives us inside information on how this took place within the Apostle Paul. He was writing to the Church at Corinth because of the obstacles and the resistance they were experiencing. Corinth was probably the most sinful city in the Roman Empire. It was laden with the sins of the human body, appetites of the flesh and sensual patterns that the Corinthian Christians were trying to deal with. Notice in verse 7, "But we have this treasure in earthen vessels." What is this treasure? It is Jesus with His life humanized in a body prepared by Mary and then planted into the spirits of men and women so that they could have divine life within their mortal frames.

Why was this necessary? So the excellency of the power may be of God and not of us, lest any should boast. Paul says, "We are troubled on every side, yet not distressed; we are perplexed, but not in despair; persecuted, but not forsaken; cast down, but not destroyed. Always bearing about in the body the dying of the Lord Jesus, that the life also of Jesus might be made manifest in our body. For we which live are always delivered unto death for Jesus' sake, that the life also of Jesus might be made manifest in our mortal flesh. So then death worketh in us, but life in you." This tells us how His life will grow and multiply and meet the problems not only of our lives, but of our day. Life swallows up death and every time Christ is revealed within you to a further degree, your new body is being formed and your old flesh is dying.

This is the hour of salvation, the hour of cleansing, the hour of the final preparation of the bride of Christ. This is the hour when you must choose which segment of the pursued generation you are going to march with, the part marked for death and judgment or the part marked for rapture. The latter is the generation being pursued with everything the Holy Spirit has been commissioned to use.

Dr. Paul G. Trulin, an ordained minister for more than fifty years, retired from pastoral ministry after having served five churches on the American West Coast. He traveled for years to minister to national leaders, pastors and believers all over the world. His books have been translated into many foreign languages to keep up with the requests for further study of his teachings on the resurrection life of Christ working within the believer's life, through the ministry of the Holy Spirit.

Dr. Trulin has received the degree of Doctor of Divinity; an appointment to Delta Epsilon Chi, the Honor Society of Christian Colleges and Universities, for outstanding achievement in Christian service; he is listed in Who's Who in Religion; he was Chaplain of the State Senate of California in 1976; he has founded several Christian Schools of Discipleship and Schools of Ministry in many nations with World Evangelism. His five books and video teaching (DVD) have been used around the world.

Dr. Paul G. Trulin is an exceptional teacher, communicating the Word of God in a practical and effective manner for application in the believer's walk. The Holy Spirit's work in the Christian's life and the revelation of the life of Jesus is the central theme in all of Dr. Trulin's books.

Dr. Trulin has trained countless leaders and pastors around the world. He went to his reward in 1997.

DR. PAUL G. TRULIN

MY BODY - HIS LIFE * †
MY BODY - HIS LIFE / STUDY COURSE
THE MAKING OF A CHRISTIAN *
THE PURSUED GENERATION
RESURRECTION LIFE
THE NEW TESTAMENT CHURCH IN TODAY'S WORLD
MY BODY - HIS LIFE / DVD (7 DISCS)
MY BODY - HIS LIFE / VHS (11 VIDEOS)
THE VINTAGE FAITH COLLECTION / DVD (14 DISCS)

DR. ALEX W. NESS

TRANSFERENCE OF SPIRITS * †
DEAR PASTOR AND CHRISTIAN WORKER
PATTERN FOR LIVING
TRIUMPHANT CHRISTIAN LIVING
THE HOLY SPIRIT VOL. I
THE HOLY SPIRIT VOL. II
THE HOLY SPIRIT / STUDY GUIDE VOL. I
THE HOLY SPIRIT / STUDY GUIDE VOL. II
KINGDOM PRINCIPLES
HOLINESS
SUFFERING
BORN AGAIN *
PIONEERING
UNTO FULL STATURE / DVD (7 DISCS)
THE VINTAGE FAITH COLLECTION / DVD (14 DISCS)

STÉPHANE CHAUVETTE

THE DEVIL'S LAST CHANCE *
WHAT A STORY! *
AS HE IS *

PRACTICAL EVANGELISM *

AS INDICATED, SOME ITEMS ARE AVAILABLE IN FRENCH * AND IN SPANISH †

PLEASE CONTACT MORIAH PUBLICATIONS INC. FOR MORE INFORMATION:
WWW.MORIAHPUBLICATIONS.COM | CUSTOMERSERVICE@MORIAHPUBLICATIONS.COM
514-951-1832